The Death of MARAT

Royal Museums
of Fine Arts
of Belgium

mare & martin

FOREWORD

In 1999, in *Farewell to an Idea,* T. J. Clark defined *The Death of Marat* or *The Last Breath* as the work through which modern art came into being, in a unique association of creative act and revolutionary commitment. Beyond its specific references, the work initiated a dynamic of breaking with the past which, almost a century later, provided the basis for the very idea of the avant-garde. Jacques-Louis David's masterpiece remains to this day a major reference in our postmodern imagination.

Entering the Royal Museums of Fine Arts of Belgium in 1893 through the bequest of Jules David-Chassagnol (1829-1886), the grandson of the painter whom he himself had not known, the canvas had already experienced the vicissitudes of revolutionary turmoil, of Napoleon I's desire to excise this turmoil from the collective memory, and of the artist's exile in Brussels after the restoration of the French monarchy. A century before this donation, which paid homage to Belgium, the country that had welcomed and given employment to the fugitive regicide, *The Death of Marat* was painted in just three months, from July to October 1793. Several replicas were made by the workshop of the artist who, in his flight, took with him the original, now threatened with destruction after it had once been honoured with a place on the tribune of the National Assembly.

Brussels gave a warm welcome to the painter, who found there a number of loyal disciples and also trained new ones, like François-Joseph Navez, in neo-classical aesthetics. *The Death of Marat* nevertheless transcends the simple credo of a return to the antique in fruitful dialogue with the work of Caravaggio or Rubens. In its economy of means, the work reflects an ability to narrate real life even in its most tenuous materials, taking the outward form of realism while testifying to an aspiration to the timelessness of myth. Hence this modernity, which Charles Baudelaire would underline in his *Musée classique du Bazar Bonne-Nouvelle.* The painting's realistic details define the passage from the anecdote to History, which the painter's genius turns into a work of edification in its conciseness and effectiveness. The poet delivers a lesson on idealism without rejecting the speed of execution, which would become the hallmark of Manet. A secular Pietà, the painting became the foundational work of a modern tradition nourished by the mystique of breaking with tradition, constituting for David the pre-condition of a liquidation of ancestral norms in favour of those now placed at the heart of a new social contract.

In this spring of 2022, on the occasion of the French presidency of the European Union, the Royal Museums of Fine Arts of Belgium are offering an unprecedented approach to David's work combining historical and contemporary perspectives with a scientific approach. The authentic painting is presented for the first time alongside three workshop replicas now conserved at the Palace of Versailles and in the Fine Arts Museums of Reims and Dijon. To 'celebrate' this unprecedented reunion, the Royal Museums have also initiated a material and technical study of David's painting, as part of the 'Face to face' research programme being carried out in partnership with the European Centre for Archaeometry of the University of Liège. Using scientific imaging techniques and non-invasive physico-chemical analyses, the research conducted by Catherine Defeyt, David Strivay and our curator Francisca Vandepitte will be the subject of a second scientific publication to appear at the end of the year to form an ensemble with the present 'Cahier'.

The modernity of *The Death of Marat*, which is of the very substance of David's work, is also echoed in the advanced technology mobilized for these laboratory studies. And it is this modernity that contemporary artists continue to celebrate today, from Gavin Turk to Jean-Luc Moerman to Ai Wei Wei to Robert Wilson, whose interpretations underline the iconic value of David's painting. But not without shifting the attention of today's spectator from Marat to Charlotte Corday, the protagonist voluntarily excluded from the painting, and of the very meaning of whose combat Rachel Labastie reminds visitors.
Thus, beyond the analyses which seek to deliver their share of knowledge, David's masterpiece has lost none of this mystery which, from Munch to Picasso, has never ceased to feed the imagination of 20th century artists before igniting that of our contemporaries. Revolution and modernity constitute two vanishing points of a perspective, certainly threatening, which both fascinates and then haunts us. David represents them stripped of all artifice, in a work which is as effective artistically as it is ideologically.

MICHEL DRAGUET

THE DEATH OF MARAT BY JACQUES-LOUIS DAVID
A fresh look at the masterpiece

CATHERINE DEFEYT
& FRANCISCA VANDEPITTE

FIG. 1
Jacques-Louis David, *The Death of Marat*, 1793, oil on canvas, 165 × 128 cm. Brussels, Royal Museums of Fine Arts of Belgium.

In his posthumously published collection 'Curiosités esthétiques' (1868), Charles Baudelaire's comments range more widely than the trendy artistic scene of 1846. Following a pleasant visit to an exhibition of neoclassical paintings by Jacques-Louis David (1748-1825), Jean-Auguste Dominique Ingres (1780-1867) and lesser-known masters at the Musée Classique du bazar Bonne-Nouvelle, Baudelaire affirmed with unexpected vigour the sincerity and rigour of French revolutionary painting. The fact of its living 'from both mind and soul' constitutes for him a commendable break with much of the art of his day. For the author of *Les Fleurs du Mal*, this would have been an unusually unequivocal expression of feelings, were it not for the fact that he calls the painting as 'bitter and despotic as the revolution that produced such art': noble simplicity and silent grandeur, indeed – but with the guillotine in the background. In his notes to *The Death of Marat*, this poet of modernity draws attention to the contemporary, realistic detail of the murder scene: 'All these details are historical and real, as in a Balzac novel. The drama is there, in all its vivid, lamentable horror, and by a strange *tour de force* which makes this painting *the* masterpiece of modern art, it has nothing trivial or ignoble about it.'[1]

Icon of the French Revolution

To the present day, *The Death of Marat* (ill.1) has enjoyed cult status as a masterpiece of modern painting. It is no coincidence that it draws crowds for the museum, continues to prompt scholars to undertake new research and inspires contemporary artists. The reasons – political, historical and aesthetic – are many and as rich as the history of this fascinating work. Considering the painting in a broader cultural context, one can even speak of a work of art that is iconic, both in the literal sense as 'image-defining', and in an extended sense as 'symbol-forming'. Simply put, David has, with verve, transformed a complex story of political assassination into a timeless image of secular martyrdom and enlightenment.

1. 'Tous ces détails sont historiques et réels, comme un roman de Balzac; le drame est là, vivant dans toute sa lamentable horreur, et par un tour de force étrange qui fait de cette peinture le chef-d'œuvre de l'art moderne, elle n'a rien de trivial ni d'ignoble.' Charles Baudelaire, *Curiosités esthétiques*, Paris, Michel Lévy Frères, Libraires Éditeurs, 1868, p. 202.

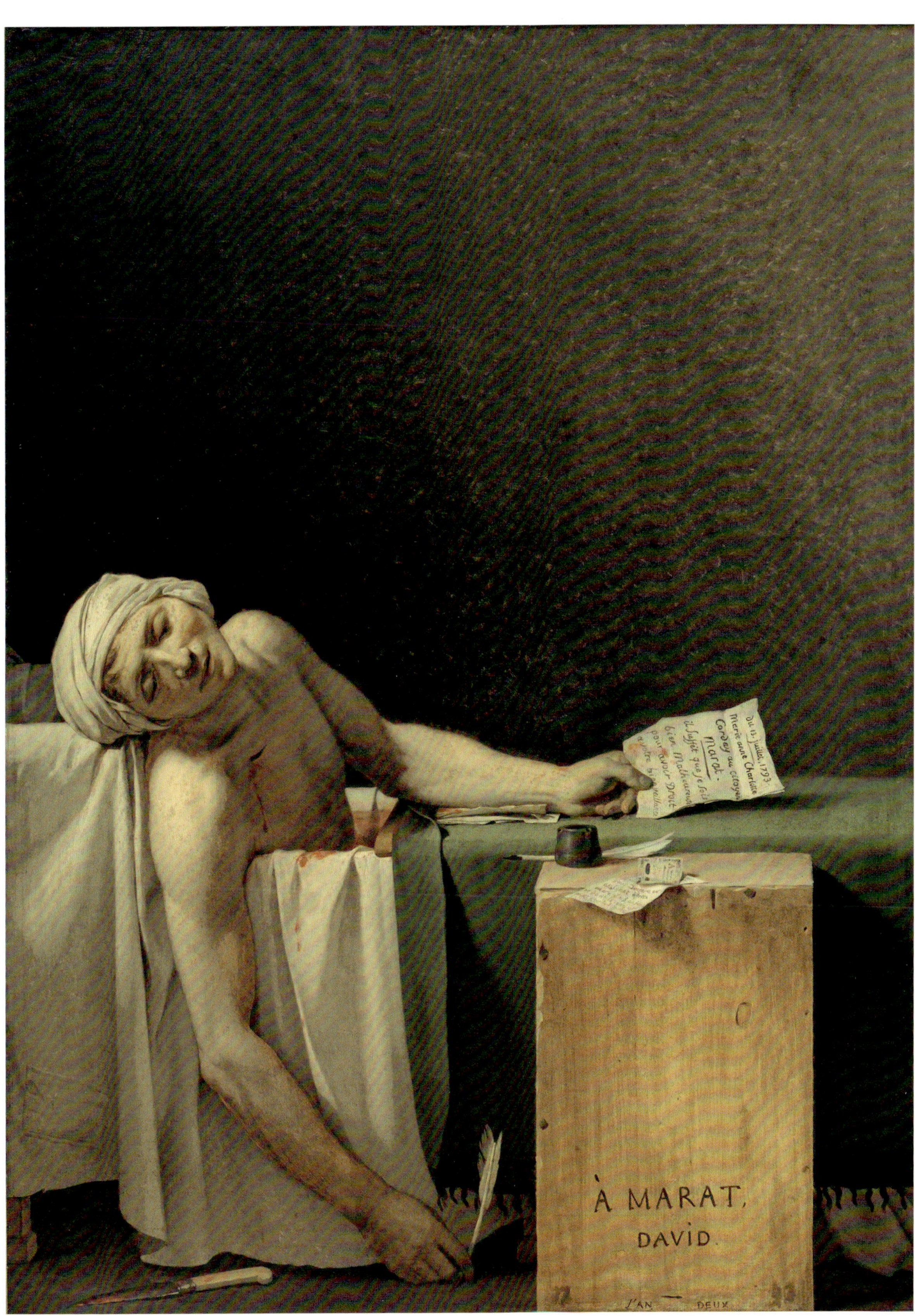
du 13. juillet, 1793.
Marie anne Charlotte
Corday au citoyen
Marat.
il suffit que je sois
bien malheureuse
pour avoir Droit
À MARAT,
DAVID
L'AN DEUX

The painting was produced between 14 July and 14 October 1793, the most turbulent year of the French Revolution. In an atmosphere of political violence, brutal terror and executions, the ideals of liberty, equality and fraternity were defended relentlessly, with a fierce counter-revolution as a bloody response. As publisher of the populace-rousing magazine *L'Ami du peuple* (founded in 1789) and a member of the National Convention, hard-line revolutionary journalist Jean-Paul Marat (1743-1793) functioned as a popular, if not formidable and hated, and pivotal figure in these upheavals.

At the end of March 1793, Jacques-Louis David sent the National Convention, of which he was a member, the first canvas of a series intended to immortalise martyrs who had given their lives for the republic. Designed for the meeting chamber of the Assemblée, they were intended to embody the ideals of the *nouveau régime*. The canvas in question, now lost, depicts the young Michel Le Peletier de Saint-Fargeau (1760-1793), a lawyer and revolutionary politician of noble birth, the first official martyr of the revolution, dying, half-naked and supported by pillows. Heroism is hard to find, but in the centre of the composition, above the deathbed, hovers a monumental murder weapon: a royal guardsman's sword cutting through a sheet of paper with writing on it. Even if *Le Peletier on his Deathbed* has disappeared without trace since 1826, a preserved drawing by Anatole Devosge (fig. 7) and an engraving by Pierre Alexandre Tardieu give us a view of the composition (fig. 6). When Jacobin Jean-Paul Marat in turn fell victim to a deadly attack on 13 July 1793, it was self-evident that David would take up the task of immortalising the political martyrdom. Thus, the genesis of the canvas was inseparable from that of the painting devoted to the death of Le Peletier. The parallels in terms of composition, structure and function are irrefutable, enabling the two works to be read as a diptych. The fact that David also staged and directed Marat's funeral, including the procession and the Republican rites – not devoid of propaganda – almost certainly contributed to the creative process. As an intimate acquaintance of the victim, and an eyewitness to the drama, David gives it an ideologically and aesthetically brilliant form. This he does in a surprisingly topical manner for a neoclassical artist from whom one might have expected a composition referring to classical antiquity or expressing the bourgeois virtues of the Roman Republic. David opts instead for the horrific historical detail, stripped of all traditional decor. 'I thought it would be interesting to show him as I found him, writing for the happiness and well-being of his people,' the artist stated.[2] He chooses a contemporary staging and shows the result of the attack, idealising the victim as an ancient hero, with references also to the iconographic topoi of the dead Christ.

But what exactly had happened on that fatal 13 July 1793 at 30, rue des Cordeliers in Paris? With a fake request for aid, a young noble royalist from Caen, Marie-Anne Charlotte Corday (1760-1793), cunningly gained entry

2. See the notice: F.L., *Jacques-Louis David, The Death of Marat* in: Museum of Modern Art, A selection of works, 2001, p.16. For an overview: Laura Malvano, *L'évènement politique en peinture. À propos de Marat par David*, in: Mélanges de l'école française de Rome, Année 1994, 106-1, pp. 33-54. For further reading: Guillaume Mazeau, *Le bain de l'histoire : Charlotte Corday et l'attentat contre Marat* 1793-2009, Seyssel, Champ Vallon, 2009.

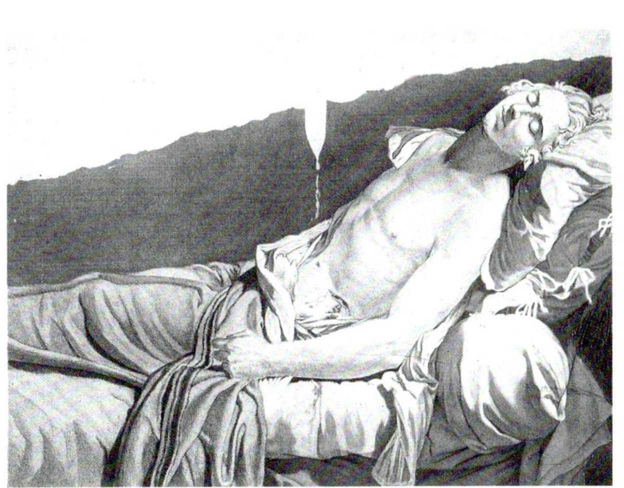

FIG. 6
Pierre-Alexandre Tardieu after Jacques-Louis David, *Le Peletier de Saint-Fargeau on his deathbed, undated,* engraving (fragment). Paris, French National Library, Department of Prints and Photography.

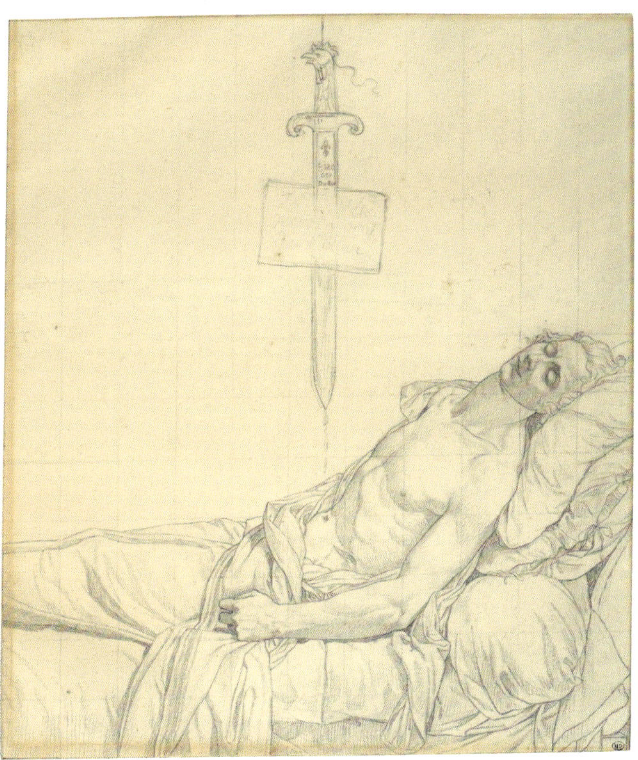

FIG. 7
Anatole Devosge after Jacques-Louis David, *Le Peletier de Saint-Fargeau on his deathbed,* pencil on paper, 38 × 35 cm. Dijon, Musée des Beaux-Arts.

to the room where Marat was bathing. Suffering from a skin disease, the pain of which was eased by prolonged baths, he had taken up the habit of working and receiving visitors during his treatment. In the painting, the dead man clutches the document with Corday's sinister plea for support in his left hand: 'il suffit que je sois bien malheureuse pour avoir droit à votre bienveillance...' (it is enough that I am deeply misfortunate to be entitled to your benevolence). Marat's response and the assignat on the wooden box that serves as a modest writing desk display the generosity that cost him his life. The naked victim hangs half-slumped over the edge of the bath, the pen still in his right hand. The bathwater is coloured red and the bloodied murder weapon, a sharp kitchen knife with which the visitor has inflicted a fatal stab in the chest, is left lying on the floor. The artist has not portrayed the circumstances or the outcome of the tragedy: the murderess, arrested immediately after the attack and guillotined after summary proceedings, is no longer even visible. The secular *Andachtsbild* shows the silence that followed the drama. The inscription in Roman letters *A Marat. David, l'an deux* lends the simple

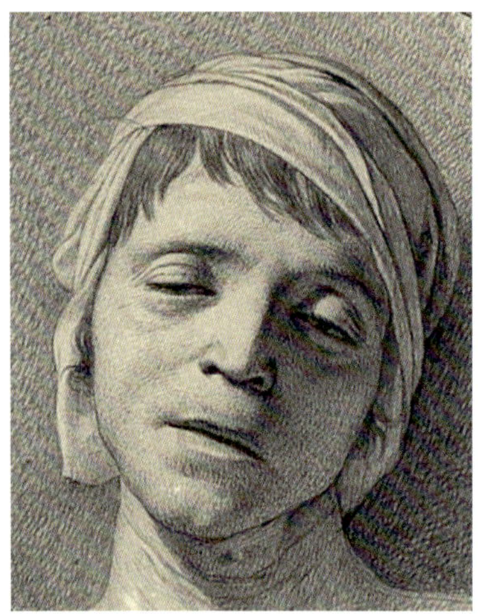

FIG. 8
Jacques-Louis David, *Study from nature of the head of the murdered Jean-Paul Marat*, 1793-1794, pen on white paper on brown paper, 33.8 × 28 cm. Musée national des Châteaux de Versailles et de Trianon.

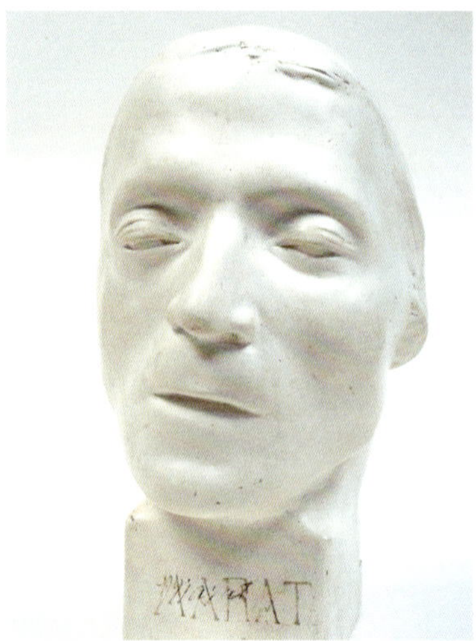

FIG. 9
Marat's death mask, [1793], plaster, 29.5 × 15.5 cm. Bibliothèque municipale de Lyon.

wooden box the significance of an antique funerary stela. The space is indefinite, the darkness tangible and the lighting dramatic. In this way the artist distances the gruesome scene from everyday life and elevates it to a timeless image of struggle, suffering and heroic death. David remembers his friend and ally as a generous hero, sincere and stern, who sacrificed his life for his revolutionary ideal.

Later the same year, when the drummer-boy Joseph Bara (1779-1793) was killed by counter-revolutionaries during an uprising in the Vendée, this evocative tragedy formed the subject of the third and final canvas of the ensemble, (fig. 10) though it would have to wait a while in the artist's studio without being completed.

On 16 October 1793, *The Death of Marat*, together with *Le Peletier on his Deathbed*, were presented to the public at a commemoration ceremony held in the Cour carrée of the Louvre. In November 1793, both works were hung in the meeting chamber of the Assemblée, on either side of the president's lectern. There they remained until February 1795, the year the Directoire came to power.

However politically agile Jacques-Louis David might prove during the Napoleonic regime, several years later the artist would be presented with the bill for his revolutionary past. As a member of the National Convention, he had, after all, taken part in the trial of the deposed King Louis XVI and voted in favour of his death sentence. When the French royal family was restored after the fall of Napoleon and the Congress of Vienna, he – 'a regicide' – fled to Brussels, where he lived and worked until his death in 1825. His revolutionary painting was brought to safety, entrusted to pupil Antoine-Jean Gros and went underground for many years. A group of young artists gathered in Brussels, including future Academy director François-Joseph Navez, with David keeping an open studio. In Brussels, David enjoyed fame, leaving such a mark on artistic life as to be called the 'father of Belgian painting'.

Since 1893, *The Death of Marat* has been a key work in the collections of the Royal Museums of Fine Arts of Belgium. David's Grandson Jules David-Chassagnol bequeathed it to Belgium in 1886, in gratitude for the hospitality extended to his grandfather during his exile.

Insight into the material, deeper than the eye can see

Four studio replicas of the emblematic revolutionary canvas are preserved – all in France – in the collections of the Château de Versailles (fig. 2), the Musée du Louvre (fig. 3), the Musée des Beaux-Arts de Reims (fig. 4) and the Musée des Beaux-Arts de Dijon (fig. 5). Recently, a smaller-sized version has been discovered, which is now part of a French private collection (fig. 11). In past decades, a number of these works were subjected to various material-technical investigations using the means and capabilities of the day.

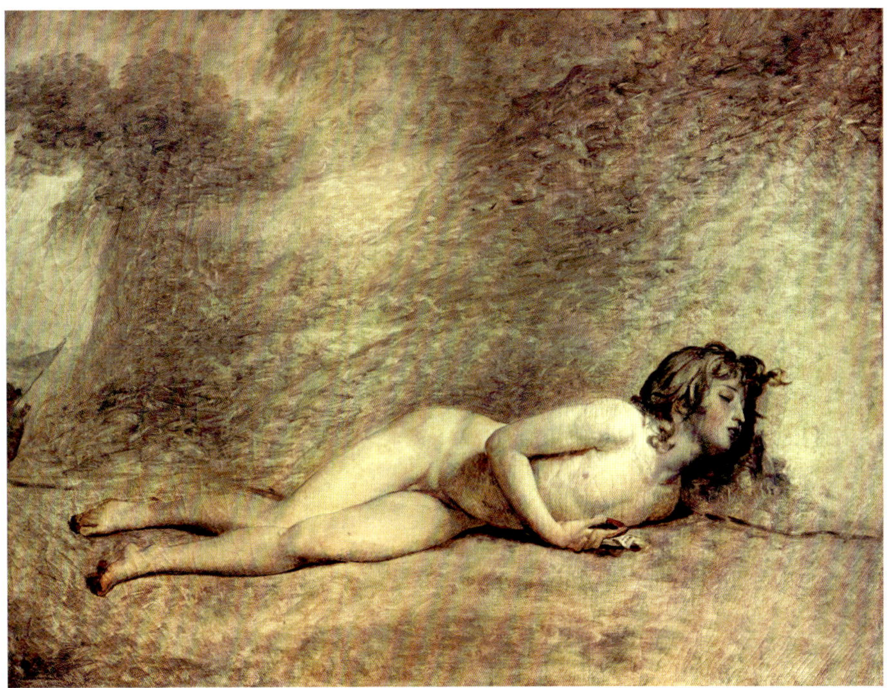

FIG. 10
Jacques-Louis David, *The Death of Bara* (unfinished), 1794, oil on canvas, 119 × 156 cm.
Avignon, Musée Calvet.

Today, the latest innovative technology now available to us provides an invitation to undertake additional in-depth and comparative research, with a view to better understanding the creative process and the biography of the work of art.

With this new research, we wish to study this iconic masterpiece through the prism of Technical Art History. This is an extension of the *Face to Face* project that seeks to apply these research methods and tools to shed new light on the representation of human faces in Western painting.[3] Less than a decade ago, this emerging heritage research discipline cautiously entered our museum galleries. Since then, the value of this cross-disciplinary approach has been widely recognized, bridging in an integrative way the gap between the thinking and working methods of traditional art-historical study and innovative high-tech research applied to cultural heritage. It is an approach that points to new avenues, deepens, refines and opens perspectives for historical and comparative research, and invites self-reflection.[4] If, in the past, there already existed a keen interest in the study of the materials and techniques in the visual arts, this research took place mainly in the privacy of the restoration studio, focused on the individual work of art, and, since it used old methods of natural science research, was viewed and taught

3. *Face to Face. Human Faces through the Prism of Technical Art History, 2019-2024*, is a Fed-tWin project, supported by Belspo, Belgian Federal Public Planning Service Scientific Policy. Promotors: David Strivay (Centre Européen d'Archéométrie, ULiège) & Francisca Vandepitte (Dep. Modern Art, RMFAB/VUB); Researcher: Catherine Defeyt (ULiege/RMFAB). For this, we would like to express our special thanks to Mr Dominique Marechal, Curator of nineteenth-century painting, for his valued contribution to the interpretation of the research results.

4. For new perspectives see: Sven Dupré, *De kunst van het maken*, Universiteit Utrecht, 2017.

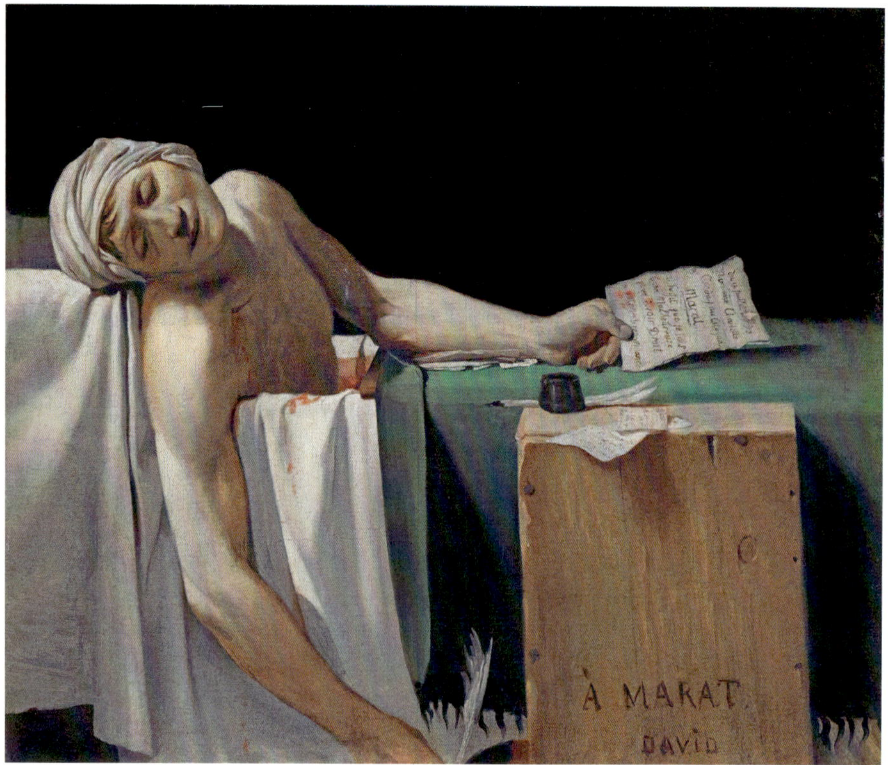

FIG. 11
Anonymous, *The Death of Marat after David,* [after 1840], oil on canvas, 72 × 91 cm.
France, private collection.

as an 'auxiliary science' of art-historical activity. The reasons for this are many. Traditionally, the emphasis in art historiography has been on archival, iconographic, biographical and literary research. As in most educational programmes, a clear distinction was made between working with the head and with the hands: between training at the university and at the academy. Thus, material-technical research has, starting from the same view of studio practice, too long been attributed a limited, supporting role in the context of preliminary research for restoration work or of attributions and expert opinions. Today, however, a turning point has been reached. With the spectacular developments of non-invasive physico-chemical research techniques and scientific imaging and their bespoke applications, this hierarchy has become obsolete. Research paths developed in dialogue are offering new keys to a better understanding of the material identity of works of art. In concrete terms, the research field of technical art history lies at the intersection of art history, science and conservation. An additional merit is that this material-technical approach to the work of art unexpectedly stimulates a holistic view of artistic creation.

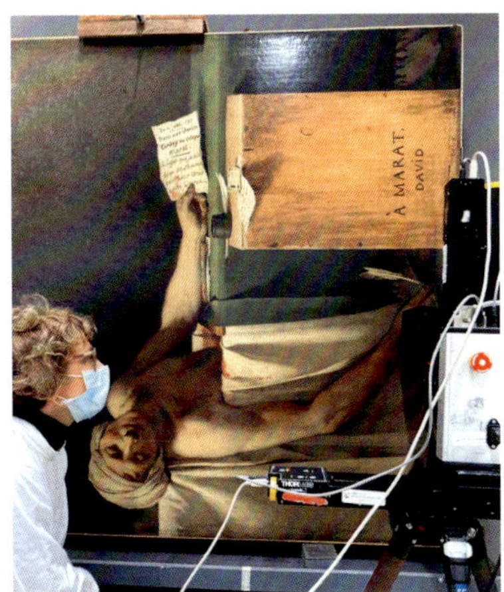

FIG. 12
Acquisition of chemical images by the MA-XRF system of the University of Liège.

Looking over the artist's shoulder

Studying *The Death of Marat* according to the principles of technical art history means in the first instance that we are seeking to understand the painting in terms of David's original intentions, his choice and use of materials and techniques, and their relationship to the very specific context of creation and possibly by extension to the perception of his contemporaries. In other words, we time-travel to the unique moment of the production of the work of art in the studio, in 1793, in order to acquire knowledge and insight into the specific creation process and the neoclassical studio practice in vogue at the time. The intended destination of the work may also merit attention. Secondarily, we shall pay attention to the biography of the work of art, its material treatment and the changes it has undergone over time. To place us in a position to interpret these, a map will be produced of all deviations, changes in structure and chemical reactions in the work of art. In this way, the researcher collects a wealth of data about the structure of the work, its composition, and its structural stability, which form the basis for his/her critical analysis. With the clinical eye of a medical physician, the researcher makes an initial diagnosis against which to test earlier statements, findings and hypotheses about the material origin and life of the work up to the present day. Quality craftsmanship and clumsy or unexpected interventions are exposed, exhibiting on rare occasions glimpses of artistic brilliance. In this way, technical art history focuses on the evolution of the work in all its complexity. Physical composition and degradation or damage in the structure of the work can be determined and older restorations detected, interpreted and possibly explained. On rare occasions, a hidden composition comes to light, by the same artist or by a different one, or the chemical composition of the materials used raises questions about the dating and authenticity of the work of art. By extension, comparative research allows us to classify and analyse the work's material-technical characteristics by school, tradition, studio practice and idiosyncrasy. *Hiding making, showing creation*[5] may long have been a widely disseminated motto in studio practice: today technological developments dissolve this dichotomy in one fell swoop. There is no doubt that *The Death of Marat*, an excellently documented masterpiece of great historical significance about which whole libraries of books have been written, which is not free from myth-making, and which is in optimal preservation condition, invites an exhaustive study on the basis of new research techniques and methods. Some recently acquired material-technical data described below are already reason to place prevailing assumptions in a new perspective.

5. See Rachel Esner, Sandra Kisters, Ann-Sophie Lehmann, *Hiding Making. Showing Creation. The Studio from Turner to Tacita Dean*, Amsterdam University Press, 2013. This publication brings together a number of studies on studio practice, the creative process and the interaction between hiding and showing from the nineteenth century to the present day.

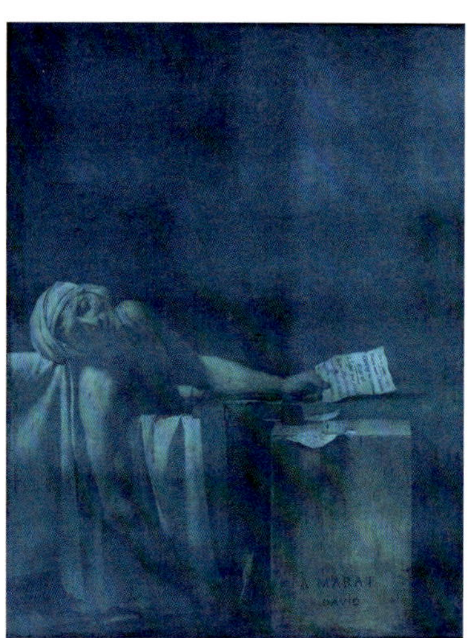

FIG. 13
Photograph of *The Death of Marat* under UV light.

The eye of technology: scientific imaging

Technical art history lies at the intersection of art history and the data provided by analytical techniques and scientific imaging. Although most of these techniques have existed for many years, recent technological developments have made it possible to miniaturise scientific instruments, making them transportable while maintaining an accuracy close to that of laboratory equipment. It is therefore no longer the work of art that comes to the laboratory but the laboratory that goes to the work of art.

Multispectral imaging, defined as the capture of the same image in several wavelength regions, is one of the most widely used technologies in technical art history. In our case, it involves acquiring an image of the painting using light sources in the visible (VIS), ultraviolet (UV), infrared (IR) and X-ray regions. The constituent materials of the paintings will react in different ways to these rays, making visible certain physical characteristics of the painting as well as its different layers, from the support right through to the varnish.

The first photograph taken uses light in the visible range with a profile similar to that of sunlight. By calibrating the colours, this photograph faithfully reproduces the appearance of the painting and serves as a reference document for other images. A photograph under raking light, i.e. by shining light on the painting sideways at a very low angle, is then used to make visible the surface condition of the painting. This serves to locate losses of quality in the pictorial layer, such as cracks, as well as deformations of the support. Illumination by ultraviolet radiation (365 nm) gives a record of the fluorescence of the painting's surface materials, making varnishes and touch-ups visible. In this study, high resolution photographic documentation was produced.

The visible light and ultraviolet (fig. 13) light images were produced using the scanning system developed by the University of Liège.[6] Each image records a 4 × 3 cm area of the painting. These images are then assembled in a panoramic view to obtain a high-definition image of several billion pixels.

IR reflectography (IRR) uses the fact that infrared radiation can penetrate paint layers through to the underlying layer, given the reduced covering power of certain pigments at wavelengths of 2 µm. Infrared light is absorbed by pigments differently than light in the visible spectrum. This light passes through many layers of paints that are opaque to visible light, but is absorbed by certain components, in particular carbon-based layers. IRR makes it possible to distinguish certain pigments by their relative absorption but also to visualise changes in composition and the preparatory drawing, which is generally in pencil (fig. 14).[7]

X-ray radiography is one of the oldest and most widely-used scientific imaging methods for examining works of art. X-rays can penetrate many materials and in this way provide a visualisation of the internal structure of an object.

6. Three-dimensional translation system equipped with a Nikon D7500 camera with an AF-S Micro Nikkor 105 mm Nikon lens and Godox LED lights.

7. The infrared reflectography was done using an Osiris camera (Opus Instruments) sensitive in the 0.9–1.7 µm range and halogen lamps.

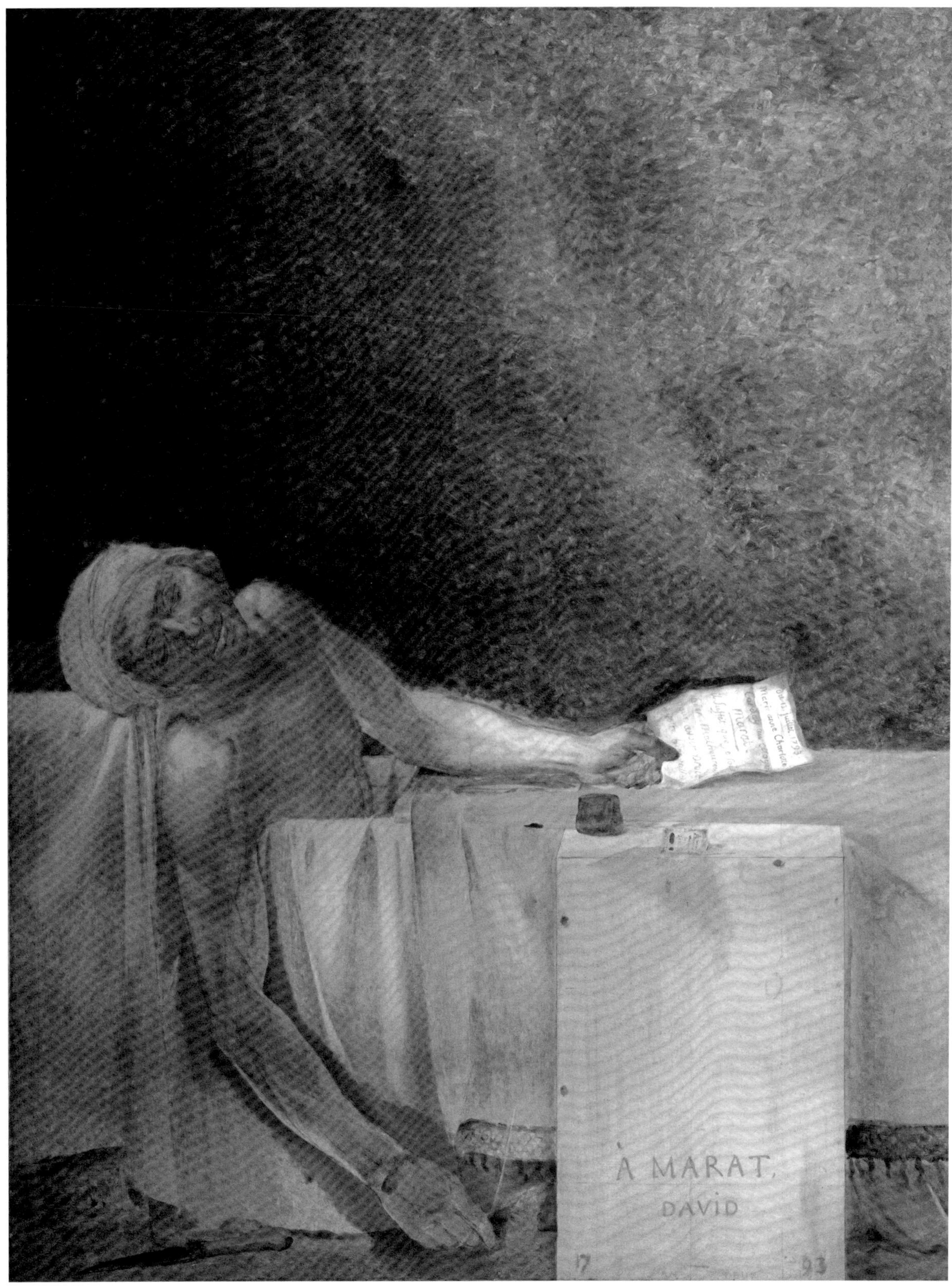

FIG. 14
Infrared reflectograph of *The Death of Marat*.

The transmission of X-rays through materials is inversely proportional to the atomic weight of the elements of the sample and to the thickness traversed. This means that only heavy elements, such as mercury or lead and, to a lesser extent, metallic elements, can absorb X-rays sufficiently to show up on an X-ray. Certain compositional *pentimenti* as well as the internal structure of the support and the frame are made visible in this way.[8]
Finally, certain areas of interest are also examined under a digital microscope (Dino-Lite) with magnifications up to 200×.

Science at the heart of artworks

The two main methods of physico-chemical analysis are X-ray fluorescence spectroscopy and Raman spectrometry.
X-ray fluorescence spectroscopy (XRF) is a non-invasive elemental analysis technique (fig. 12). It permits the qualitative and semi-quantitative analysis of chemical elements with an atomic number greater than 15 (that of phosphorus), even when present only in very small quantities. An excitation source consisting of X-rays irradiates the surface, causing an X-ray fluorescence spectrum to be emitted. The physical phenomenon of X-ray fluorescence consists of a secondary emission of X-ray photons resulting from the ejection of an electron from an internal orbit of an atom. As the energy levels of the emitted rays vary with the chemical element, the X-ray fluorescence spectrum obtained makes it possible to identify or even quantify the chemical elements constituting the work being analysed.
During a measurement, a specific area of the painting is irradiated with X-rays and the intensity of the emitted X-rays is recorded. The resulting signals can be assigned to specific elements and the elements in turn to specific pigments; for example, mercury can be associated with vermilion. Recently, instruments have appeared with which it is possible to scan the whole painting to arrive at a complete analysis of the chemical elements for the entire work. In this way one can record the intensity of the X-rays for each specific energy (and therefore for each element) on the surface of the entire painting. The XRF scans of the painting were produced using the system developed by the University of Liège.[9]

Raman spectroscopy is a molecular analysis technique that uses light scattering. Only a very small part of the incident light is scattered by the object, and Raman spectroscopy uses only a small fraction of this scattered light.
This light scattering takes two different forms. Most of the scattered light does not change its wavelength during the process: such scattering is known as elastic scattering or Rayleigh scattering. However, a small part of the scattered light undergoes a change in its wavelength. This scattering is known as Raman scattering or inelastic scattering.

8. The X-ray radiography was performed using a mobile digital radiography system with a 40 kV X-ray source and a CCD detector from X-Ris.

9. The XRF was used in imaging mode using the system developed by CEA consisting of a Moxtek Magnum X-ray tube (50kV) (with an Ag anode), an Amptek X-123SDD detector (25 mm^2), with a resolution from 130 eV to 5.9 keV and our translation system. The tube was set to 40kV with a current of 120 µA. The resolution is 1mm. The scanning speed is 4mm/s. The spectra were processed using PyMCA software.

This change in the wavelength of the scattered light occurs because the energy of the incident light causes changes in the vibrations of the molecules. The frequencies of such vibrations depend on the molecule's structure, which means that each molecule scatters incident light in a different way. This molecular analysis technique is complementary to elemental analyses by X-ray fluorescence spectroscopy, and provides information on the organic and inorganic materials encountered in the pictorial environment. In this way it is often possible to identify binders, varnishes and pigments which cannot be identified or discerned by X-ray fluorescence. Identification is generally by comparison with reference spectra.[10]
The data and images were all acquired on the museum site using the mobile laboratory.

The immortalised face: the creative process

A certain mystery surrounds the process by which this particular masterpiece was created, on the one hand because it was realised in a very short time (three months), and on the other hand because of the squaring grid discovered under the layers of paint during a first technical examination in 2000. Squaring is a technique that allows the transfer of a drawing or a composition onto another support, with or without a change of scale. By breaking down shapes and lines into smaller sections, it permits the proportions to remain the same.[11]

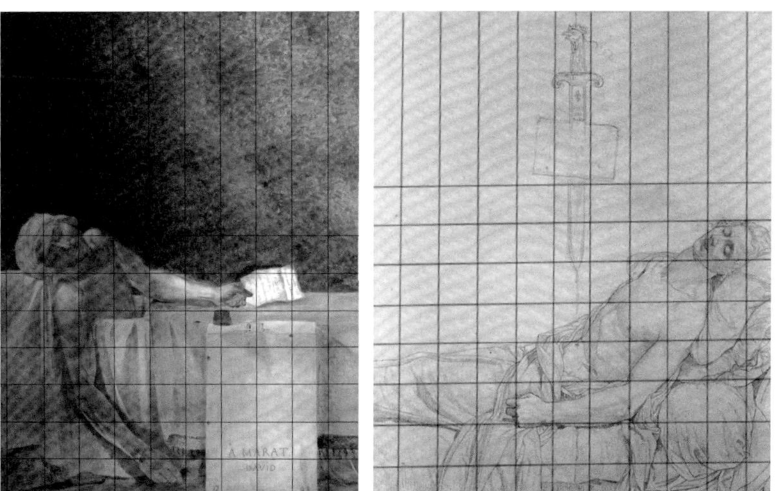

FIG. 15
X-radiograph of *The Death of Marat* and Devosge's drawing with the squaring accentuated.

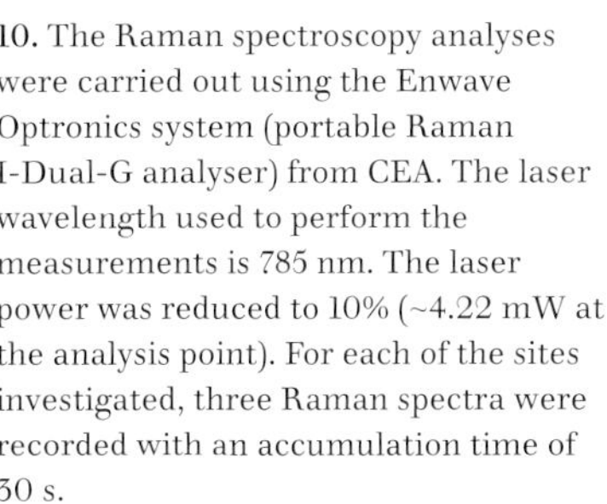

10. The Raman spectroscopy analyses were carried out using the Enwave Optronics system (portable Raman I-Dual-G analyser) from CEA. The laser wavelength used to perform the measurements is 785 nm. The laser power was reduced to 10% (~4.22 mW at the analysis point). For each of the sites investigated, three Raman spectra were recorded with an accumulation time of 30 s.

11. Ségolène Bergeon-Langle and Pierre Curie, *Peinture et dessin. Vocabulaire typologique et technique*, Paris, Éditions du Patrimoine, 2009, p. 234.

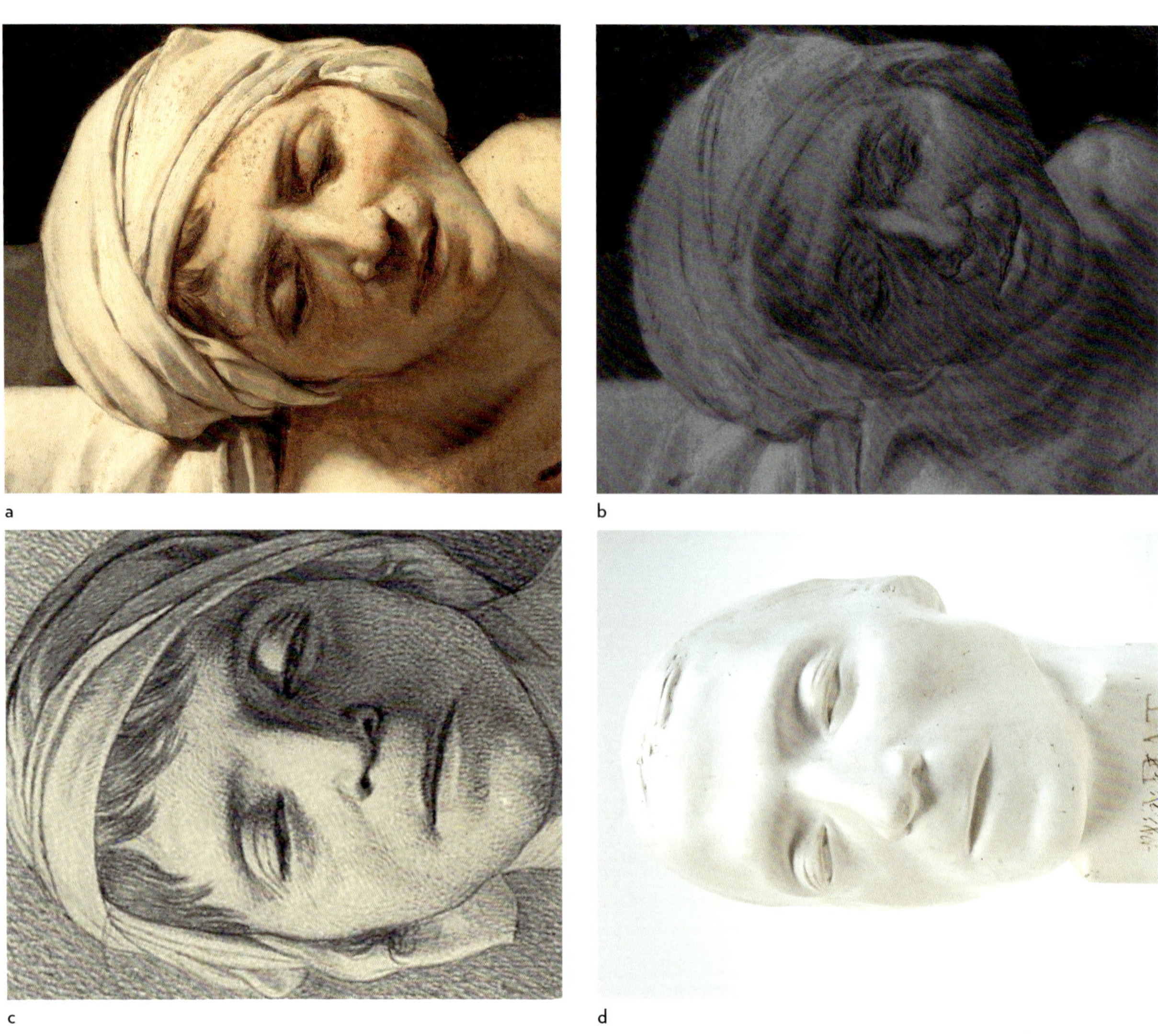

FIG. 16
Comparison of the visible (a) and infrared (b) images of the pen drawing *Study from nature of the head of murdered Jean-Paul Marat* rotated 100° (c) and the death mask rotated 90° (d).

The use of this method implies the existence of a model. The question of the identity of this model remains as yet unresolved. However, the results of the recent IR reflectography examination have led to the formulation of a new hypothesis. Specifically, a correspondence was established between the grid drawn on *The Death of Marat*, visible in IR, and the grid displayed on the drawing of Lepeletier. This drawing, depicting Lepeletier on his deathbed, was created by Devosge, a pupil of David, from a painting by the master, commonly considered the sister work to Marat [fig. 5]. We know from archival documents and historical testimonies that the painting of Lepeletier, which vanished and has not been seen since 1826, and the one of Marat were of the same dimensions and intended to be seen together. In light of these facts, the same squaring shown in the drawing of Lepeletier could have served also for the realisation of the painting of Marat, in particular for maintaining the proportions between the two martyr figures depicted by David.

Next, the painted head of Marat, whose rapid brushwork recalls the unfinished self-portrait with a palette executed in 1794 (fig. 17), seems to have little in common with the detailed pen-and-ink study *The Head of Dead Jean-Paul Marat* (fig. 8), made from life or from a death mask taken – it is said – by Mme Tussaud (fig. 9). David in fact paints Marat's head in the opposite direction to his drawing. Likewise, the half-closed eyes and hanging mouth of the drawing are clearly distinct from the painting. We also observe a reversal in the positioning of highlights and shadows. Louis Hautecœur is one of the first authors to have underlined the close link that exists between the painted head and this study of Marat's head.[12] Indeed, superposing the images of the two heads shows that the orientation of the head in the painting is aligned with the drawing when rotated approximately 100 degrees to the left (fig. 16c). This simple operation highlighted the almost perfect match in terms of the facial oval. Indeed, the shape of the painted face seems borrowed from the drawing. There are other intriguing correspondences between the two figures, such as the positioning of the eyes, mouth, nose, and part of the turban. In the painting, the left-hand part of the cloth wrapped around the head of the deceased has been considerably thickened. This increase in volume lends realism to the orientation of the head.

The newly acquired high-resolution IRR image has revealed the presence of *pentimenti* in the eyes, mouth and lower jaw area (fig. 16b). Indeed, the eyes seem to have been initially represented open more widely than they are in the visible image, i.e. more similar to the eyes in the drawing. Additionally, the IRR examination supports the hypothesis of the use of Marat's death mask to model lights and shadows (fig. 16d). On the one hand,

12. Louis Hautecœur, *Louis David*, Paris, Editions de la Table Ronde, 1954.

the dysmorphism of the left-hand part of the face visible in the preparatory drawing, consistent with the death mask and the physical description of Marat by his contemporaries, is not represented in the *Head of the Dead Jean-Paul Marat*. On the other hand, the heavily marked shadow under the nose in the preparatory drawing seems consistent with the use of a 3D model like the plaster death mask from Lyon Library. In conclusion, David could have used both his detailed drawing and the death mask to immortalise Marat's face. The comparative analysis of the IRR images with preparatory sketches and a possible plaster model enable us to follow the artist's reasoning and movement in the creation of his work of art. It was no strange *tour de force*, but rather a creative work by a privileged witness – rapid, contemporary, and yet deeply rooted in neoclassical aesthetics and studio practice.

The palette revealed

In addition to these findings, the MA-XRF method rendered visible the distribution of the inorganic pigments that David used in portraying *The Death of Marat*. David's palette is typical for the late eighteenth century. Indeed, the different pigments identified by analytical methods are those commonly used by most painters of the time. The turban that girds Marat's head, the bloody sheet, the two quills and the paper documents contain mostly white lead pigment. This is an inorganic pigment used by artists since Antiquity, and which remained until the nineteenth century one of the only white pigments offered to painters by colour manufacturers, before being gradually replaced by less toxic pigments like zinc white and titanium white. Lead white is also found in the skin tones of the dead Marat, where it is mixed with other pigments in varying proportions. For rendering the flesh, David used at least five different pigments: lead white, Naples yellow, red vermilion, carbon black and one or more iron (hydr)oxide pigment(s) such as earths and ochres.

Like lead white, the other pigments identified in the skin tones were used elsewhere in the composition. Red vermilion, present in low concentrations for the flesh colours, is the main pigment used to imitate the colour of blood. Vermilion (cinnabar) is a mercury sulphide (HgS), its oldest form being the finely ground mineral cinnabar. Mercuric sulphide can also be produced artificially. This pigment has been used from ancient times to the present day. However, examination under UV light of the blood covering the knife blade and its analysis by Raman spectroscopy revealed the addition of red lake.

The background of the painting is painted using *frottis*, as is often the case with David, based on the juxtaposition of brushstrokes split and oriented

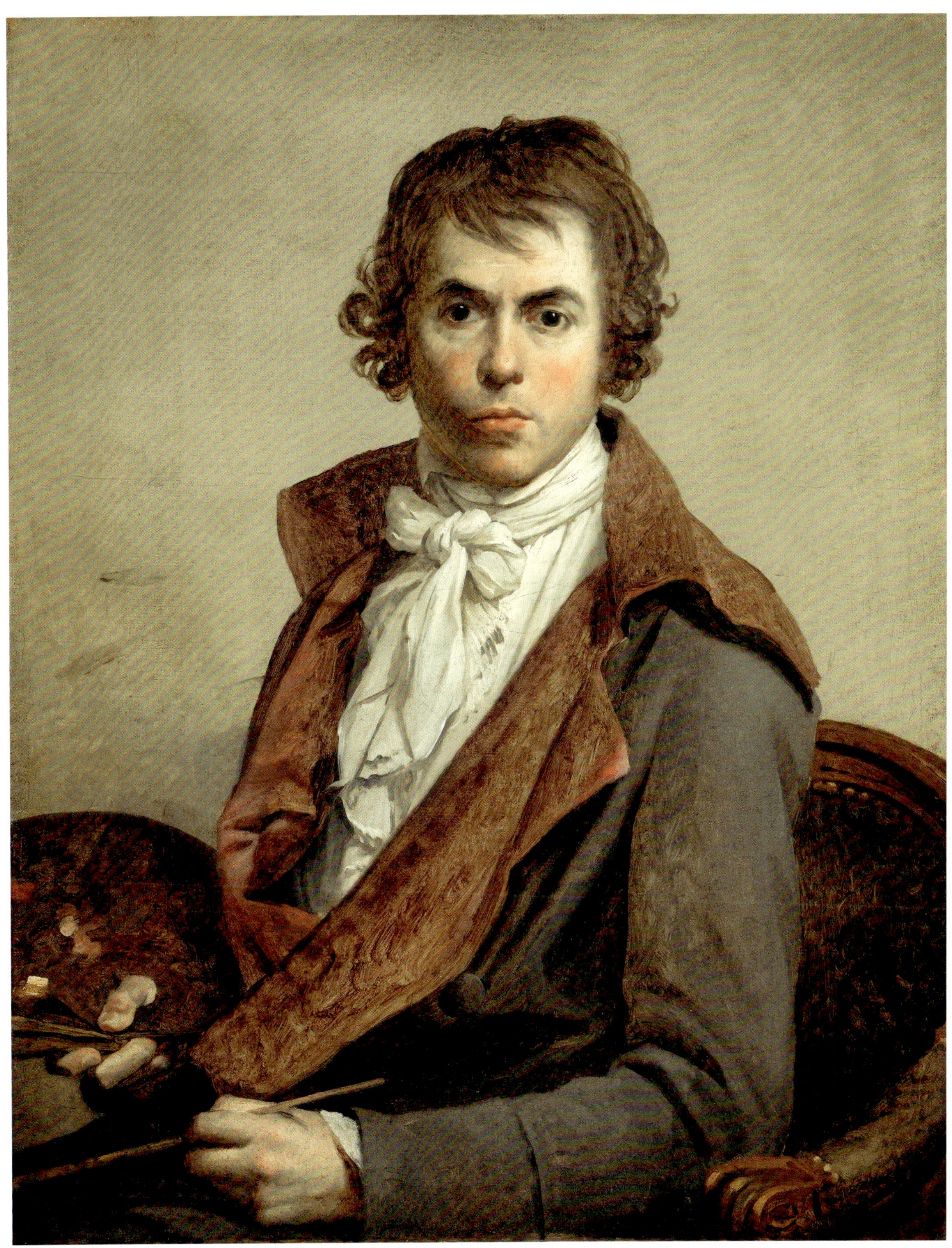

FIG. 17
Jacques-Louis David, *Self-portrait with palette*, 1794, oil on canvas, 81 × 64 cm. Paris, Musée de Louvre.

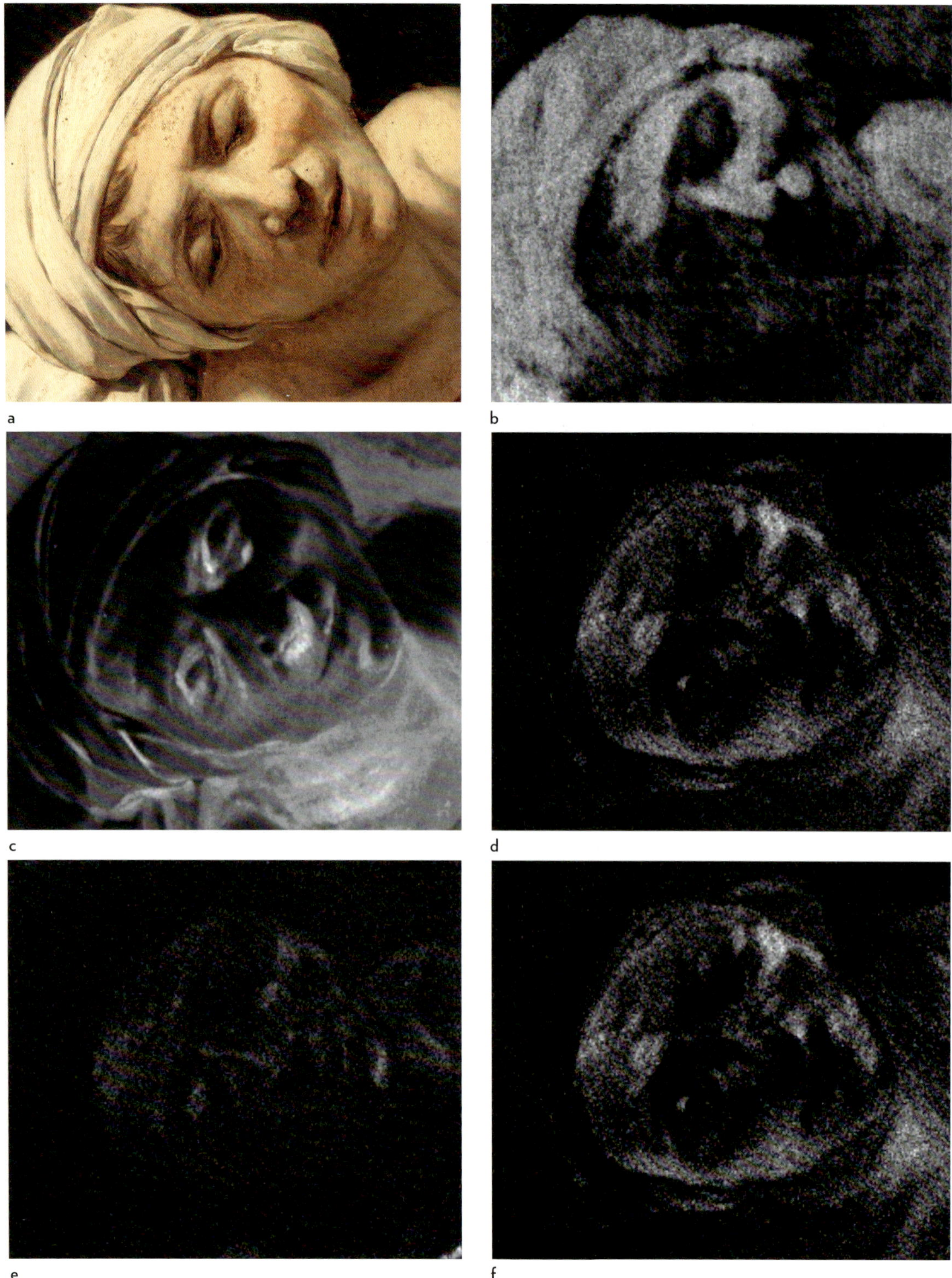

FIG. 18
Comparison of the visible photograph (a) with the chemical images obtained by MA-XRF for lead (b), iron (c), calcium (d), mercury (e) and antimony (f). The concentrations are proportional to the grey levels.

differently depending on the location. The *frottis* applied to the background consists mainly of iron (hydr)oxides and carbon black, and is particularly legible in IR reflectography. Carbon black is the common name for a black pigment, traditionally produced from carbonised organic animal or vegetable matter such as bone or wood. It has many different names, each reflecting a traditional method of production. Charcoal sticks have been used by artists for drawing throughout the ages. The same material is used today in toners for photocopiers and laser printers.

The green colour of the blanket (fig. 19b) derives primarily from mixing a yellow pigment, in this case Naples yellow, with a blue pigment, having an iron content compatible with Prussian blue. As with the skin tones, the grains of Naples yellow contained in the green paint layer appear distinctly in the photomicrographs. The use of compound greens, that is to say greens obtained by combining yellow and blue pigments, is a common practice in painting. Naples yellow is one of the oldest synthetic pigments, being lead antimonate $Pb_2Sb_2O_7$, but its composition may vary depending on its method of preparation. It was used until the mid-nineteenth century, after which, owing to its toxicity, it was gradually replaced by cadmium yellow in particular. Prussian blue is a complex inorganic ferrous salt discovered in 1704. The overall formula is usually written as $Fe_4[Fe(CN)_6]_3 \times H_2O$.

The ensemble of pigments identified by the analytical methods perfectly reflects David's palette as described by Jean-Pierre Thénot in 1847:[13]

13. Jean-Pierre Thénot, *Les Règles de la peinture à l'huile: dédiées à son ami et élève M. Raffort*, Paris, Chez Danlos, 1847.

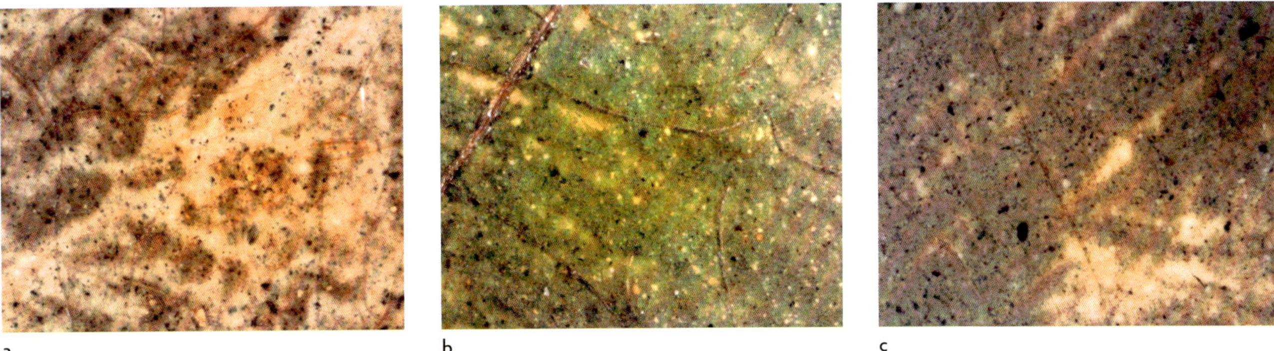

a b c

FIG. 19
Microscope image (×200) revealing the pigment grains of the face (a), the green cloth (b) and the scumbling background (c).

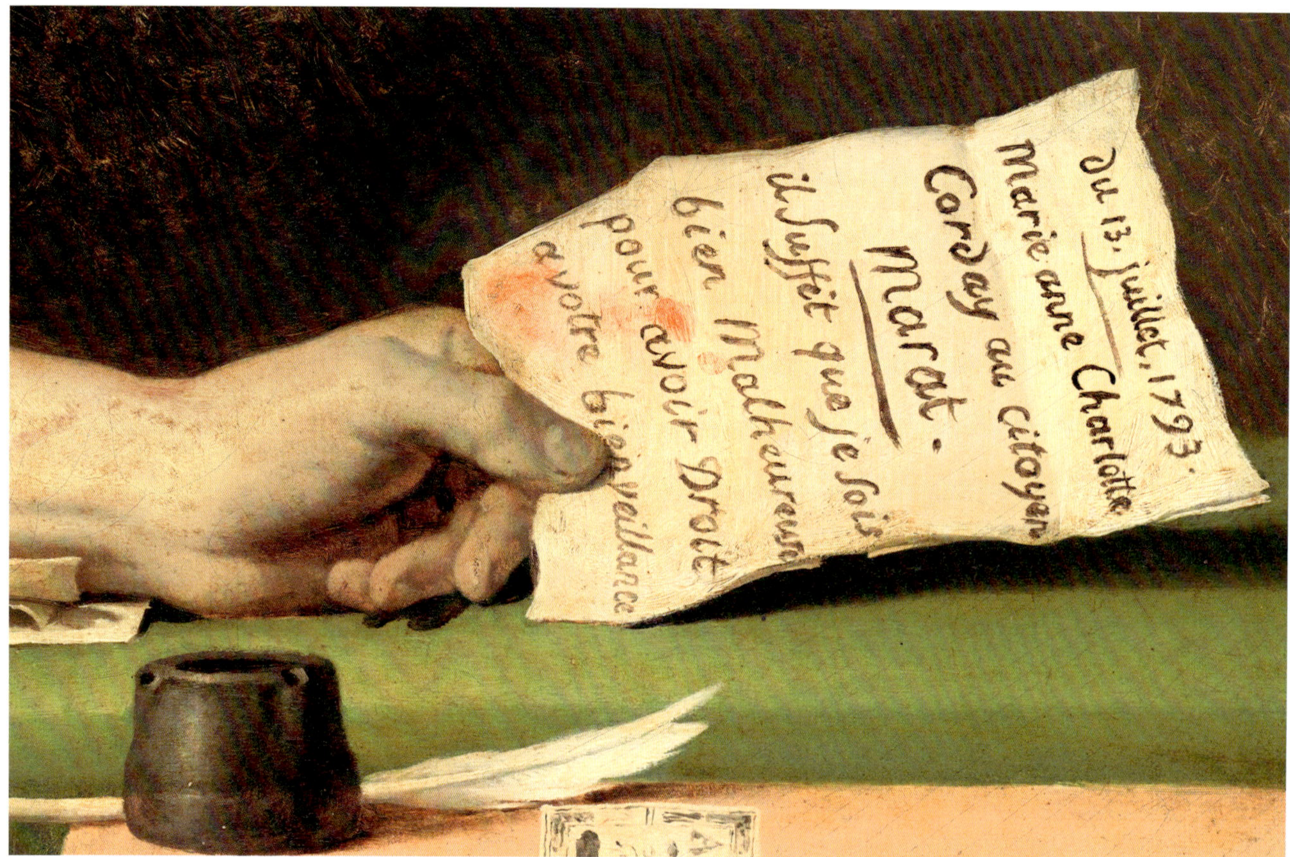

FIG. 20
Jacques-Louis David, The *Death of Marat*, detail of the left hand and the letter.

David's palette, order of colours from the thumb outwards: lead white, Naples yellow, yellow ochre, brown ochre, Italian ochre, red brown, burnt Sienna, fine carmine lake, Cassel earth, ivory black, peach or vine black. Indiscriminately Prussian blue, ultramarine blue, mineral blue, then he placed cinnabar and vermilion below these colours. Towards the end of his career, he added chrome yellow and chrome red to his palette, solely for painting draperies.

These results represent only part of the research carried out on *The Death of Marat*. Many questions still remain to be elucidated, such as the inversion of Marat's position, certain compositional changes, and again the subterfuge used to hide the masterpiece during David's years of exile.

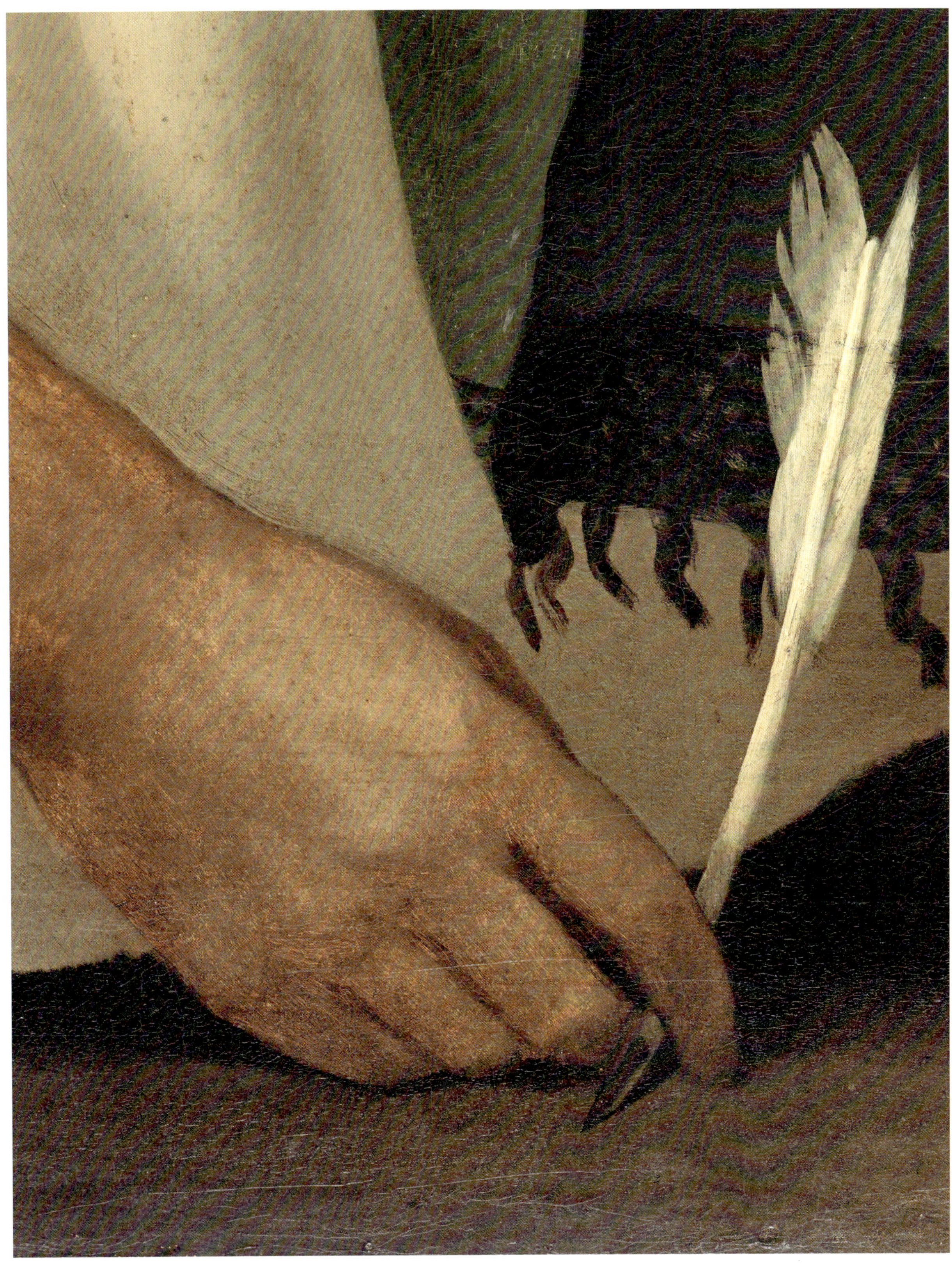

FIG. 21
Jacques-Louis David, The *Death of Marat*, detail of the right hand.

FROM SYMBOLS TO EXPRESSIONS OF SOCIO-POLITICAL DEMANDS

Modern and contemporary interpretations of the painting

PIERRE-YVES DESAIVE

FIG. 22
Jean-Luc Moerman, *The Death of Marat*, 2021, print on Chromalux, 150 × 110 cm. Private collection.

The opening of the Museum of Modern Art in 1984 was accompanied by the publication of two inventory catalogues of the Royal Museums of Fine Arts of Belgium collection, one devoted to 'ancient painting', the other to 'modern painting'. The latter volume[1] starts, for all practical purposes, with *The Death of Marat*, painted by Jacques-Louis David in 1793 [fig. 1]. It may seem anachronistic to associate a painting from the end of the eighteenth century with modern art, but chronological classification frequently displays its limits when we approach a non-standard work or artist. Baudelaire himself wrote of 'David's masterpiece and one of the great curiosities of modern art'. Above all, he was enraptured by the 'extreme speed' at which the painter worked, a trait rarely associated with neo-classical painting, and which is far from obvious to anyone looking at *The Death of Marat*. Such speed is, on the other hand, inseparable from the work of Édouard Manet, the 'first of the moderns' (to use the title of an exhibition dedicated to him at the Musée d'Orsay in 2011), whose closeness to Baudelaire is well known. Commissioned from David in July 1793, *The Death of Marat* was delivered barely three months later: by omitting to mention this historical fact, which indeed attests to a great speed of execution, the poet pretends (involuntarily?) to see this solely from contemplating the painting. Is this in order to make it more 'modern', like a work by Manet?

In the eyes of today's viewer, the "modernity" of *Marat* lies more in its composition, marked as much by the disproportionate place given to empty space, which borders on the limits of figuration, than by the manner in which it was painted. From the early twentieth century, the painting's singularity found echo with artists who were seeking a new formal vocabulary. This led to multiple reinterpretations, such as the three versions Edvard Munch (1863-1944) produced in 1906-1907 [fig. 24]. Into them the artist projects his own anxieties, depicting the violent argument with his mistress during which he was wounded in the hand by a revolver shot. A quarter of a century later, Pablo Picasso (1881-1973) also turned to David's painting to represent himself as the

1. Phil Mertens (dir.), *Musées royaux des Beaux-Arts de Belgique. Département d'Art Moderne. Catalogue inventaire de la peinture moderne*, Brussels, Royal Museums of Fine Arts of Belgium, 1984, 800 p.

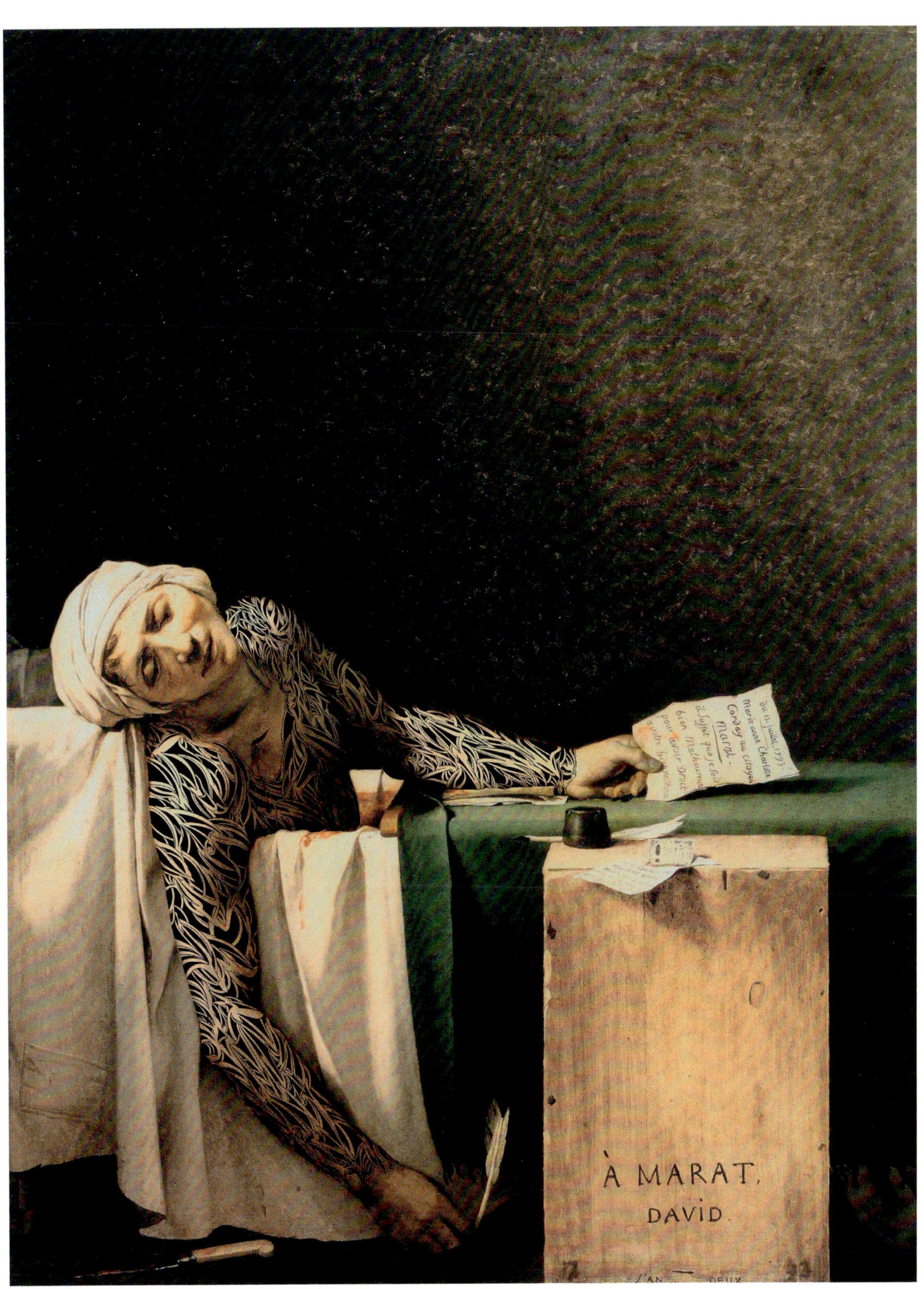
À MARAT,
DAVID

victim of the vindictiveness of a woman – in this case his wife Olga – whom he transforms into a sprawling monster emerging from behind a door (*La Femme au Stylet*, 1931 [fig. 25]). Picasso's work testifies to his subtle understanding of the colours used by David: if he associates blood red with the French flag in a fairly conventional way, the dominant colour in the composition is green, a colour very present in *The Death of Marat* and which, in the eighteenth century, was always symbolically linked to instability, but also to fate. He took up the subject again in a print and several drawings following his separation with Olga, the latter continuing to embody the murderess, and the role of Marat falling this time to Picasso's mistress Marie-Thérèse Walter [fig. 23 and 26].

The connections between David's painting and more recent reinterpretations take very divergent paths. Picasso and Munch, and after them Bernard Buffet (*The Death of Marat*, 1977) and Valerio Adami (*Marat assassiné*, 1982), bring into the image the figure of Charlotte Corday, notably excluded from the original work, but confine her to the role of the woman through whom violence and death occur. Was she a murderess, or a heroine determined to sacrifice herself to put an end to the Terror? The debate is not new, but today tends in favour of the second reading – all political considerations aside.

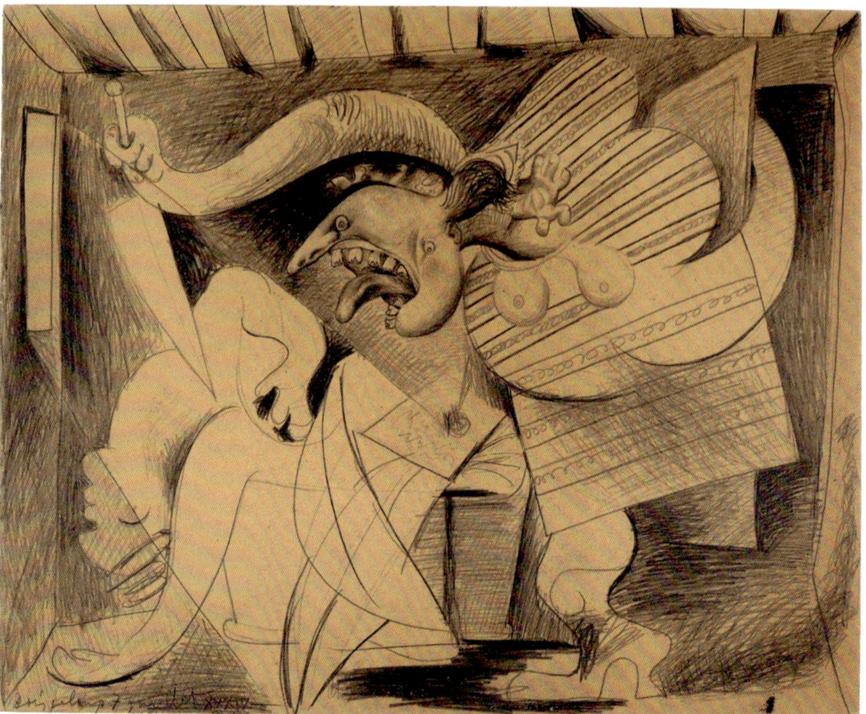

FIG. 23
Pablo Picasso, *The Murder*, 1934, graphite on thick cardboard, 40.2 × 50.6 cm. Paris, Musée National Picasso.

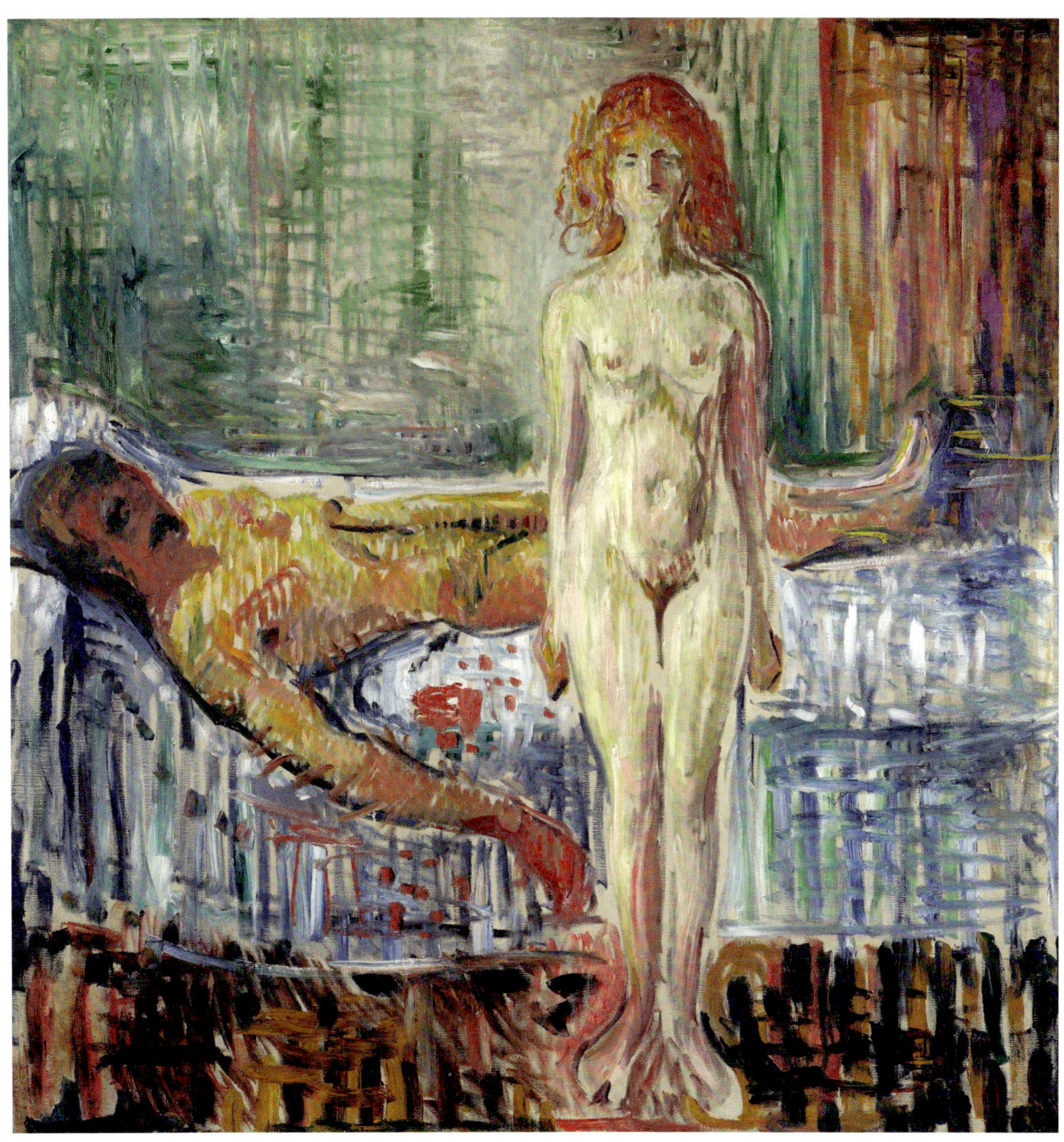

FIG. 24
Edvard Munch, *The Death of Marat II*, 1907, oil on canvas, 153 × 148 cm. Oslo, Munch Museum.

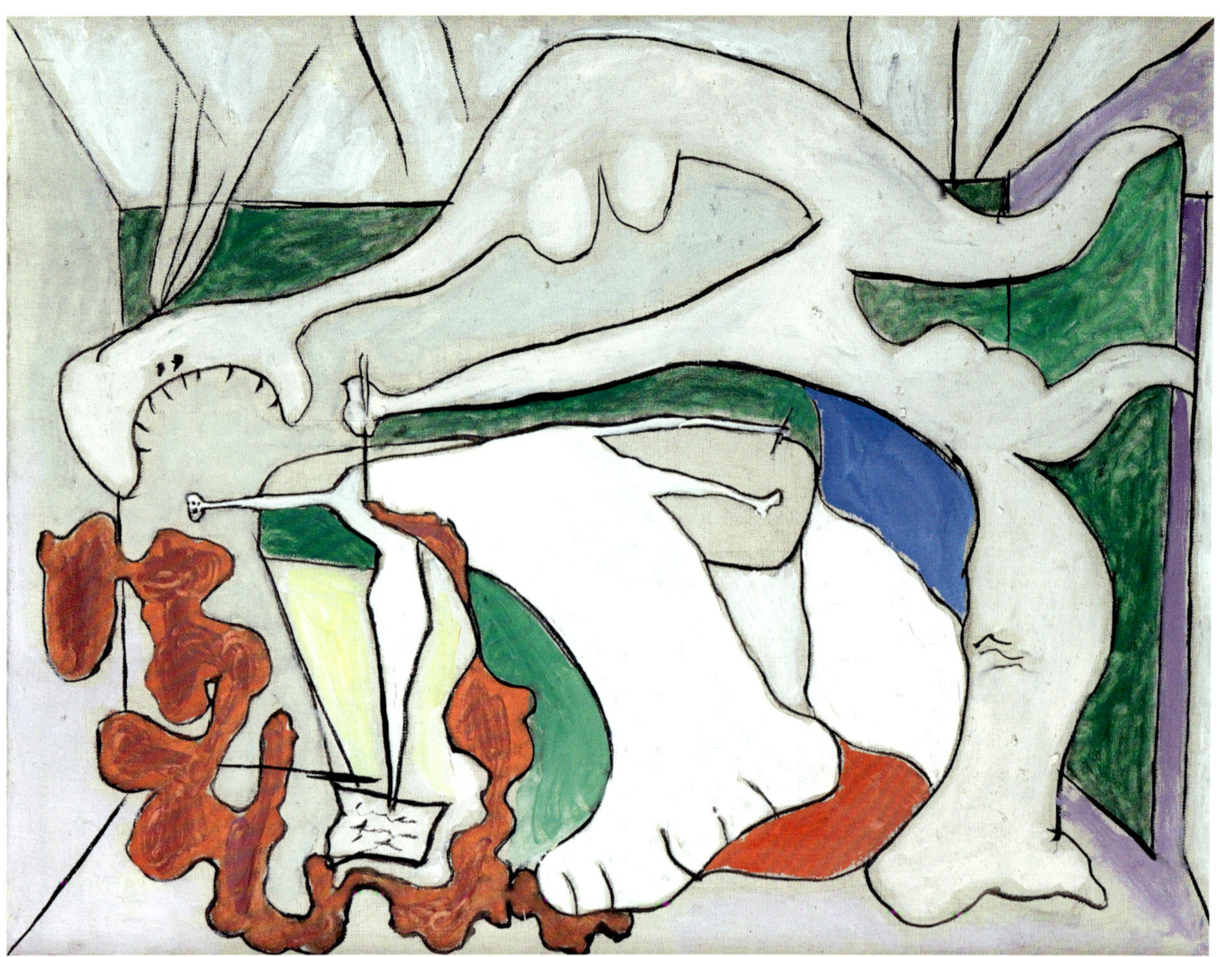

FIG. 25
Pablo Picasso, *La Femme au stylet*, 1931, oil on canvas, 46.5 × 61.5 cm. Paris, Musée National Picasso.

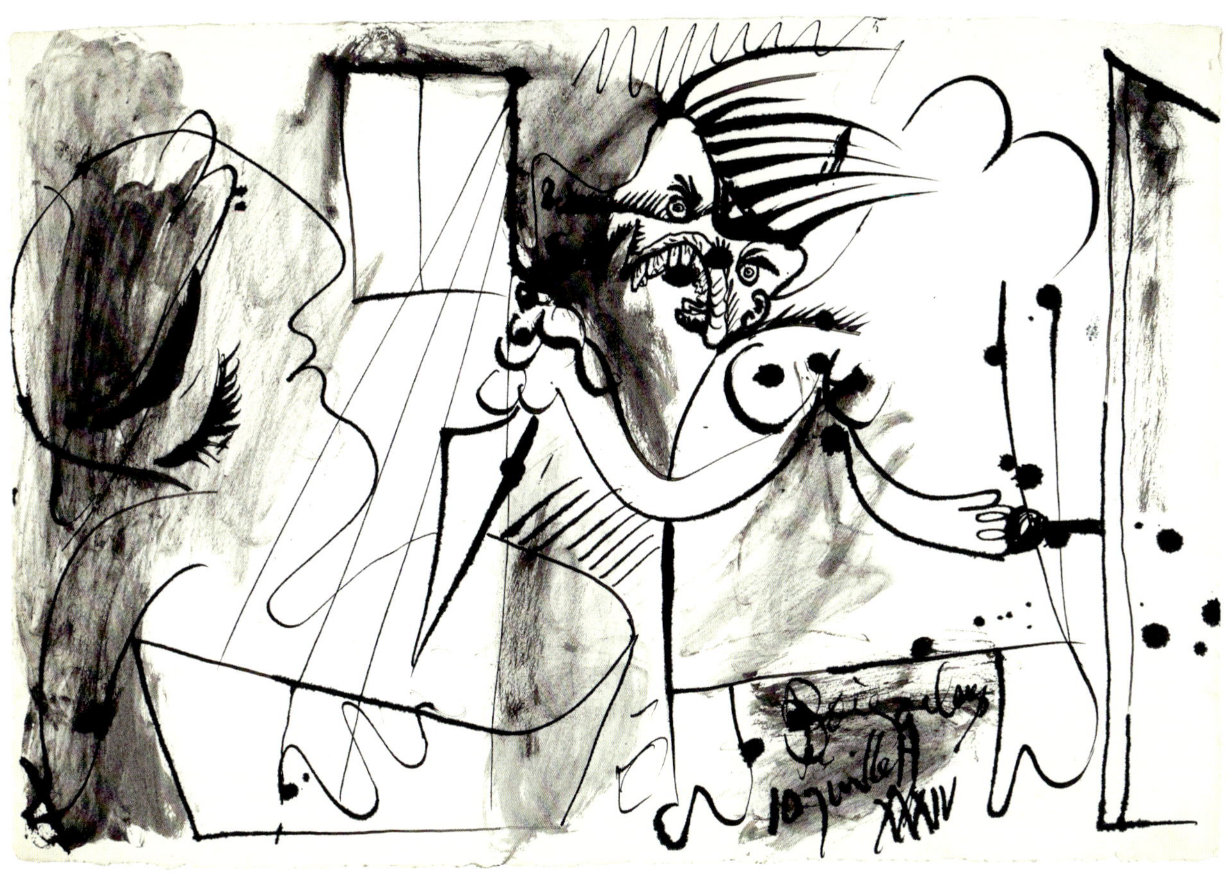

FIG. 26
Pablo Picasso, *The Murder*, 1934, pen, India ink and wash on laid paper, 34.5 × 51 cm. Paris, Musée National Picasso.

If our day is more inclined to rehabilitate Charlotte Corday, this is also because she symbolises the determination of a very young woman in the face of the blindness of a power embodied by a man. Rachel Labastie (°1978), when she was invited as part of an exhibition of her works[2] to design a work that resonates with the collections of the Royal Museums of Fine Arts of Belgium, chose *The Death of Marat*, but with the aim of creating a monument in memory of Charlotte Corday [fig. 29]. The installation takes the form of a large, stylised jewellery rack, from which hangs a white ceramic chain, fitted with both shackles and two medallions – one depicting Marat's murderess, the other her signature. The artist reproduces here a portrait drawn by Pierre-Michel Alix (1762-1817), to whom we also owe the effigy of Marat, produced in the same year 1793.

Among many others, Alix portrayed young Joseph Bara, a martyr of the Revolution killed at the age of fourteen, to whom Ian Hamilton Finlay (1925-2006), himself fascinated by the revolutionary period, devoted a minimalist *Monument*, composed of a column shaft representing a drum topped with two bronze drumsticks [fig. 28]. Finlay also designed a small sculpture, possibly the prototype of a monumental piece never made, in memory of Charlotte Corday [fig. 27]. An obelisk – a reference to that in the Place de

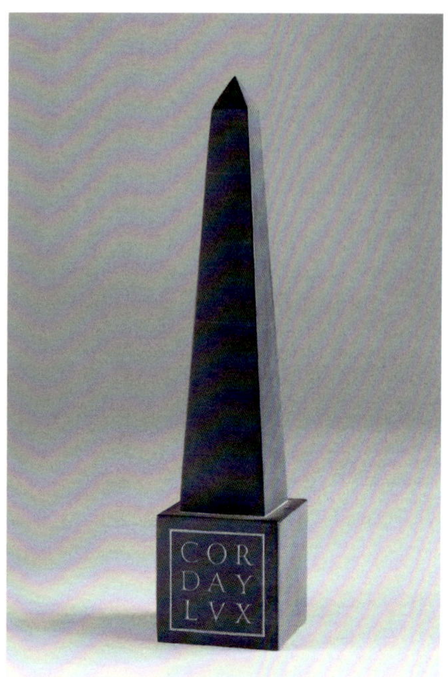

FIG. 27
Ian Hamilton Finlay, *Corday Lux*, 1989, shale, 40 × 10 × 10 cm. Abbot Hall Art Gallery, Kendal.

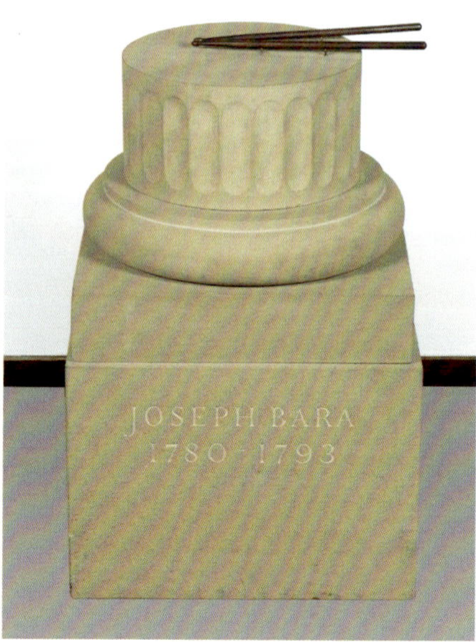

FIG. 28
Ian Hamilton Finlay, *Monument to Joseph Bara*, [1986], stone and bronze, 88.4 × 59.6 × 58.6 cm. Brussels, Royal Museums of Fine Arts of Belgium, inv. 11051.

2. *Remedies. Rachel Labastie*, Brussels, Royal Museums of Fine Arts of Belgium, 15 October 2021 – 13 February 2022 [exhib. cat. : Paris, Liénart, 2021].

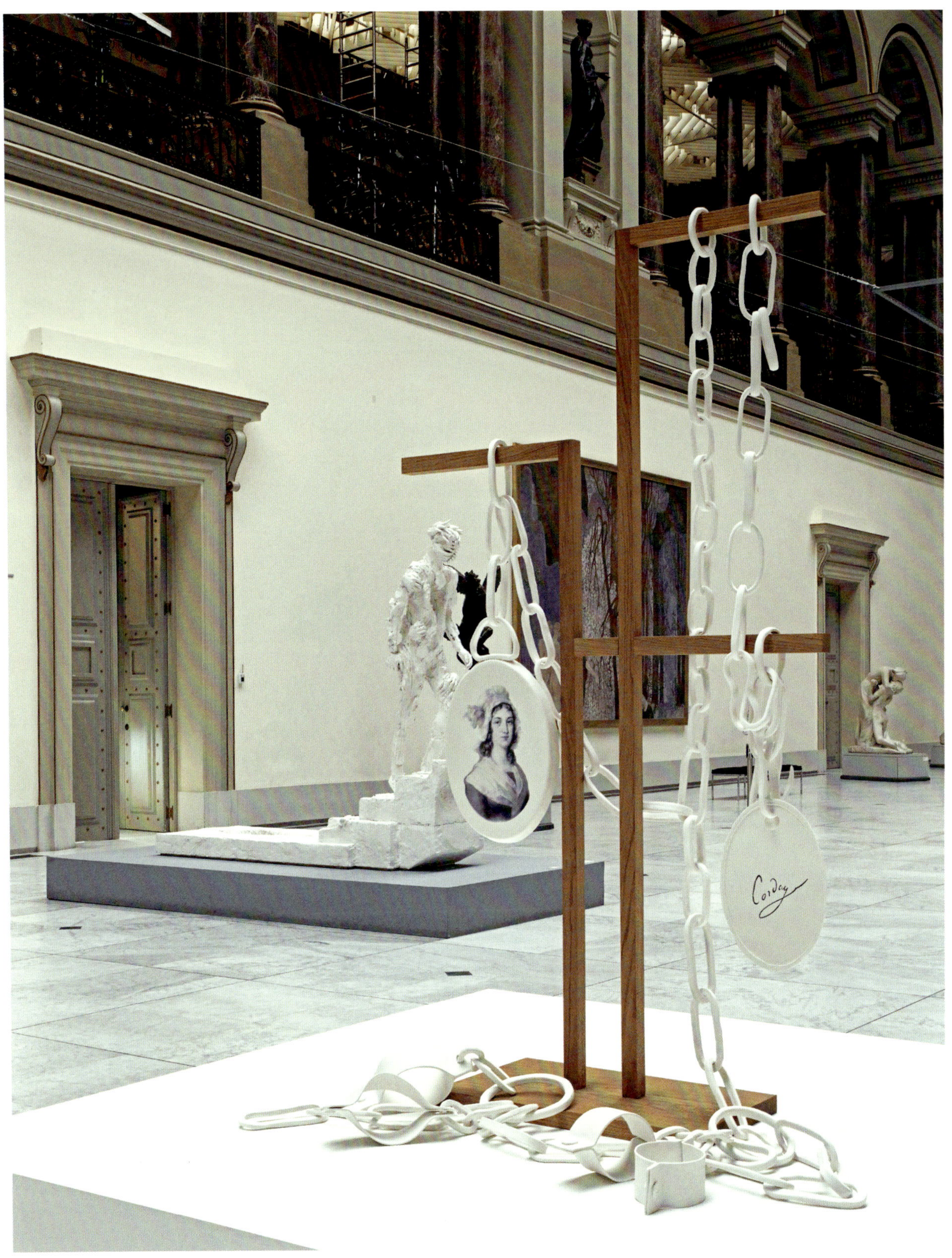

FIG. 29
Rachel Labastie, *Charlotte*, [2021], porcelain cameos and chain, oak jewellery stand, 190 × 115 × 50 cm. Courtesy of the artist.

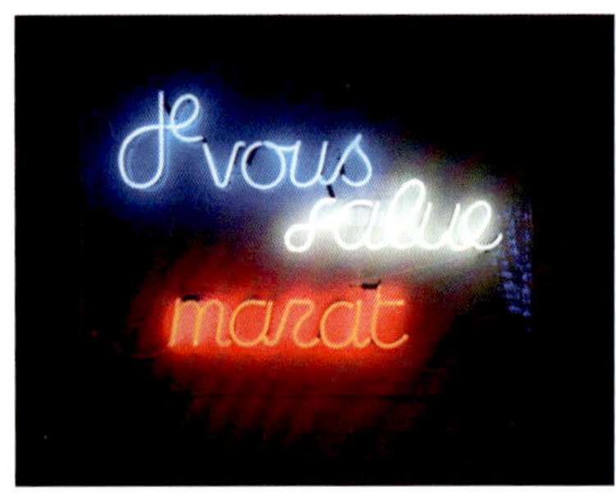

FIG. 30
Ian Hamilton Finlay, *Je vous salue Marat*, 1989, neon, 91 × 112 × 8 cm. Tate Gallery, London.

la Concorde, formerly called the Place de la Révolution, where she was executed – is placed on a base in which are engraved the names 'Corday' and 'Lux', an allusion to the revolutionary Adam Lux, who expressed his admiration for Marat's murderess, and went so far as to suggest that a statue of her should be erected, but who was guillotined shortly after she. By associating the word 'lux' with the name of Charlotte Corday, perhaps Finlay also wanted to suggest the appearance of light in a period which is among the darkest of the Revolution? Be this as it may, it is with light (neon) that he pays a vibrant tribute to Marat, albeit laden with ambiguity: 'Je vous salue Marat' (Hail Marat), in the colours of the French flag [fig. 30].

In opposition to Finlay's conceptual approach, Gavin Turk (°1967) employs a hyper-realism characteristic of his artistic practice, which he many times associates with self-portrait. Thus, he presents a life-size Marat/Turk, at rest in a bathtub – a showcase resembling an item of neoclassical furniture [fig. 32]. The effigy is in wax, in reference to the famous Marie Tussaud who claimed in her memoirs to have made Marat's death mask at the request of Jacques-Louis David himself, a story now afforded little credibility by historians [fig. 9]. Shortly after the creation of this work (1998), Gavin Turk was asked what was for him the most striking image of the twentieth century; he produced, following the same principle, a sculpture representing himself in the guise of Che Guevara, as photographed on a stretcher immediately after his execution – another martyr of another revolution. Gavin Turk's *Marat* is presented in mirror image to David's painting – the victim is here on the right side – but it is not a mirror reflection of the scene: the pen, the knife, the letter, the blood, all the constituent elements of the story have disappeared. The artist does not seek to transpose *The Death of Marat* into three dimensions, but plays at reproducing the scene, taking several liberties, such as using a bathtub which bears little resemblance to the one in which 'the friend of the people' died. To convince oneself of this, one has only to go and see the original object, which eventually ended up in the Musée Grévin, where it is exhibited today as part of the 'tableau' depicting the murder of Marat.

The list of examples of the use of Jacques-Louis David's *Death of Marat* in contemporary artistic productions grows longer by the year. The above-mentioned works stem from a sort of fascination for this fragment of history, for the characters who embodied it, and for their tragic fates. Other artists, such as Vik Muniz (°1961), Richard Jackson (°1939) and Thomas Houseago (°1972) [fig. 31], have chosen to confront their own pictorial practices through David's subject. Gavin Turk himself, a past master in the art of quotation (see his two sculptures in the Magritte Museum, inspired by the painter's famous 'Cow' period), has used images from his *Marat* to make a canvas à la Andy Warhol

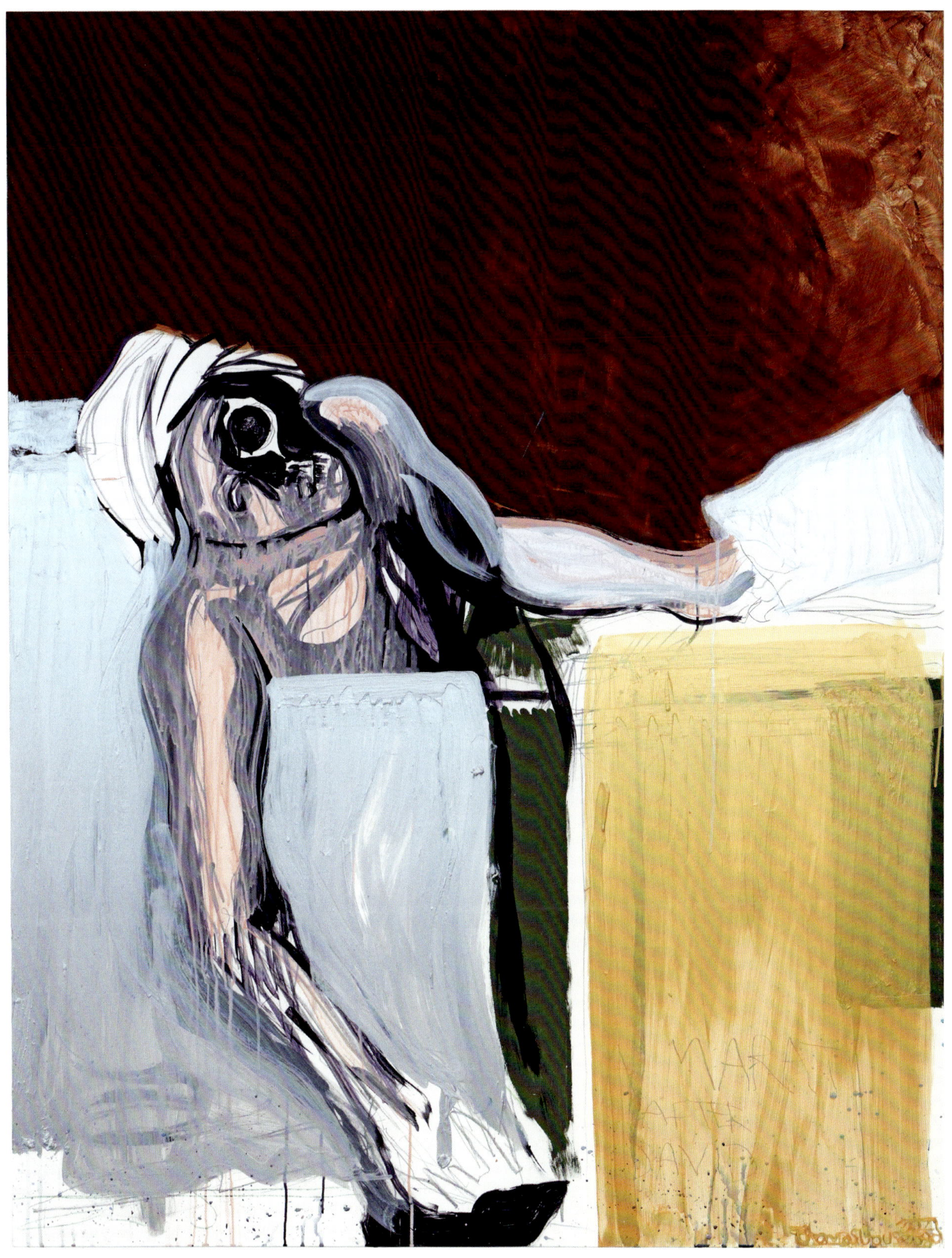

FIG. 31
Thomas Houseago, *Vision Painting – Death of Marat I after David – Malibu*, 2021, acrylic on canvas, 162.6 × 127 cm. Courtesy of the artist.

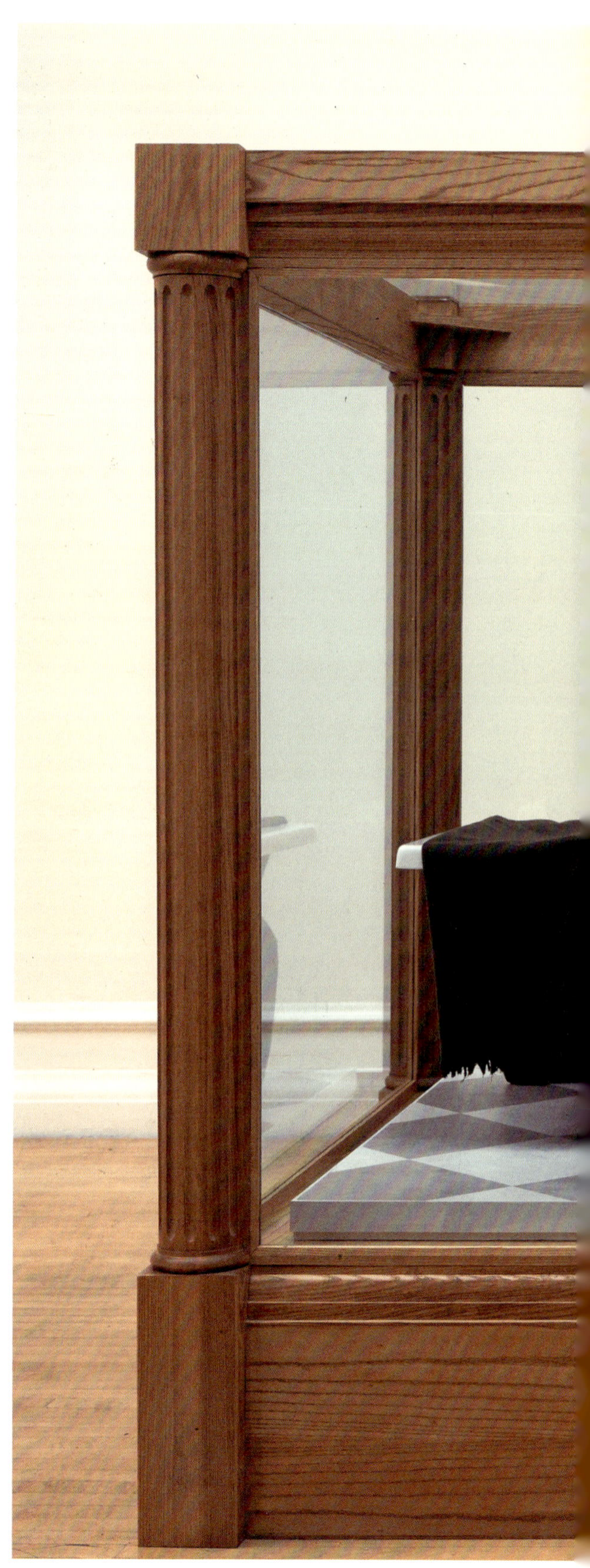

FIG. 32
Gavin Turk, *Death of Marat*, 1998,
wax sculpture, stone, wood and glass case,
200 × 170.2 × 250 cm. Private collection.

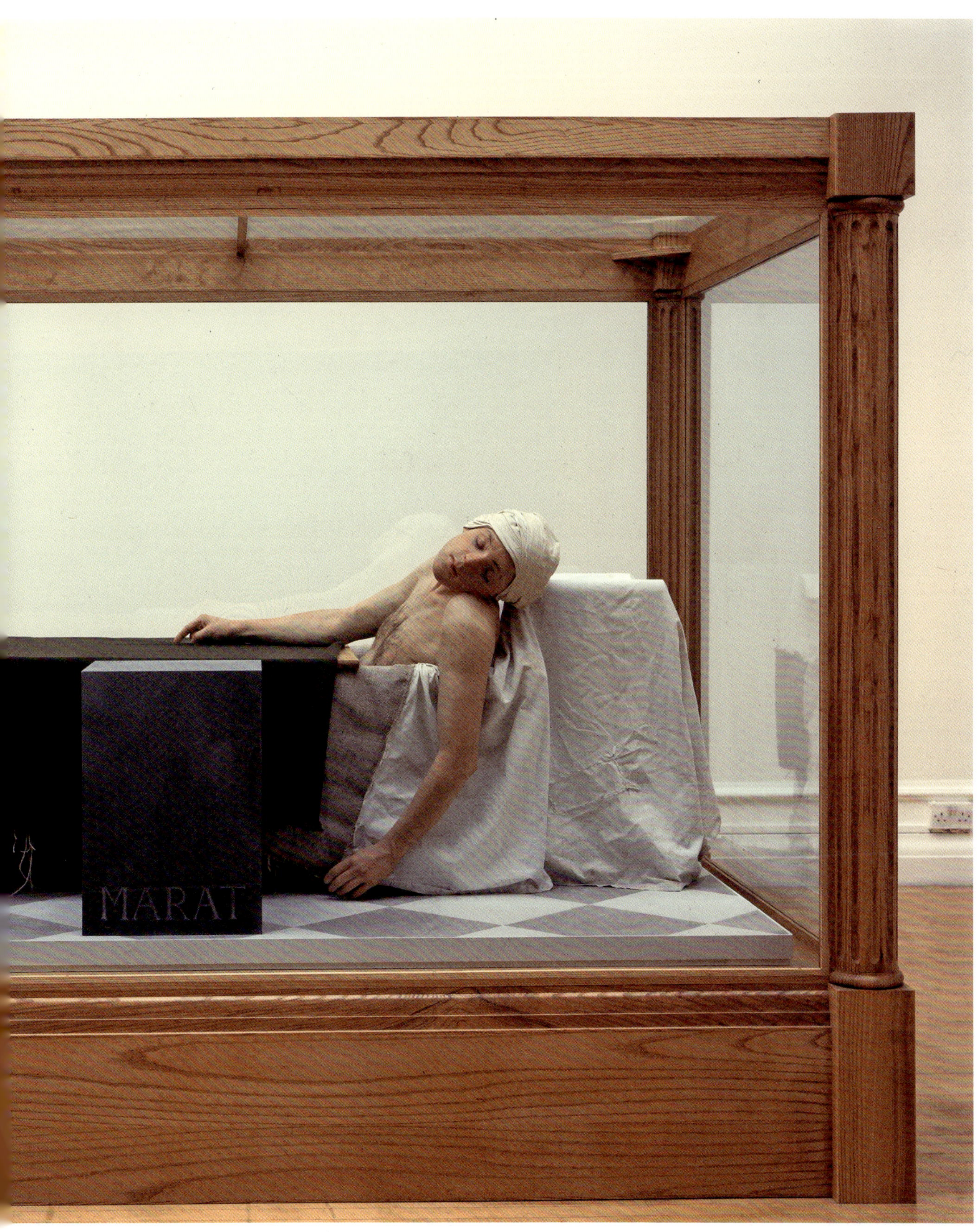
MARAT

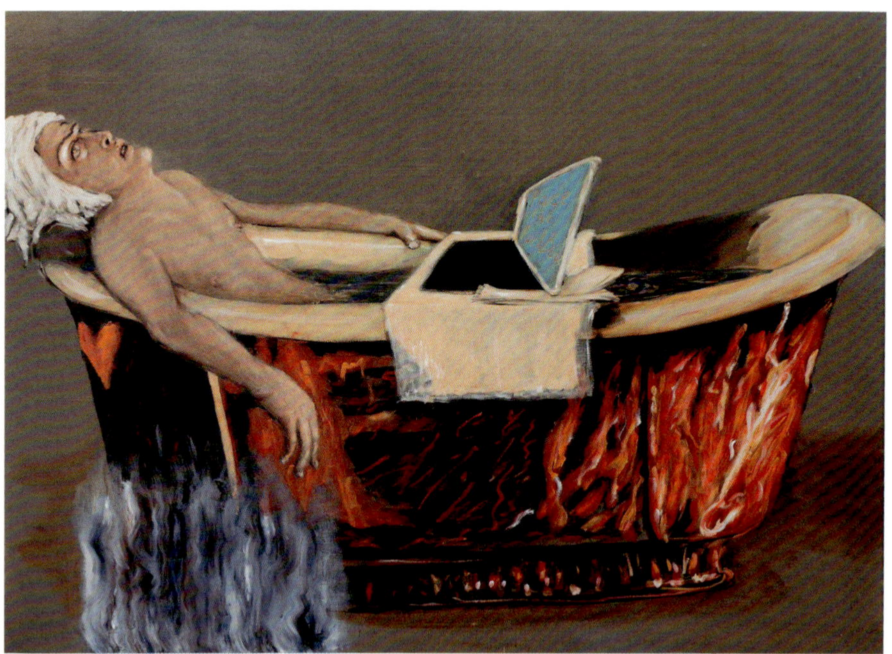

FIG. 33
Jan Van Imschoot, *La Pénétration inédite*, 2018, oil on canvas, 150 × 170 cm.
Courtesy of the artist and Galerie Templon.

(*Marat Pale Blue*, 2016). The Royal Museums of Fine Arts of Belgium also own a work by a pioneer of the Italian Transavanguardia, Ernesto Tatafiore (°1943), simply titled *To Marat* [fig. 34] which testifies as much to his taste for words as it does to his interest in the history of the French Revolution. We should also mention Jan Van Imschoot (°1963), Jacques Lennep (°1941) and Jean-Luc Moerman (°1967), who have each found in David's painting the opportunity to develop their offbeat views of the history of Western art [fig. 33, 40 and 22].

But David's painting is above all a political gesture, and the message it delivers about the violence inherent in the revolutionary quest for freedom continues to resonate with artists today. Rising to fame in the 1990s with his *Great Criticism* series of works combining the logos of well-known Western brands with Maoist propaganda posters, the Chinese artist Wang Guangyi (°1957) has repeatedly treated the theme in a manner close to geometric abstraction (*Post Classical Death of Marat A* and *B*, 1987). In turn, his compatriot Yue Minjun (°1962), one of the best-known contemporary Chinese artists on the international scene, presented in 2002 a version of *The Death of Marat* in which the main character has purely and simply disappeared, a thinly-veiled evocation of political purges as practised in dictatorial regimes [fig. 35].

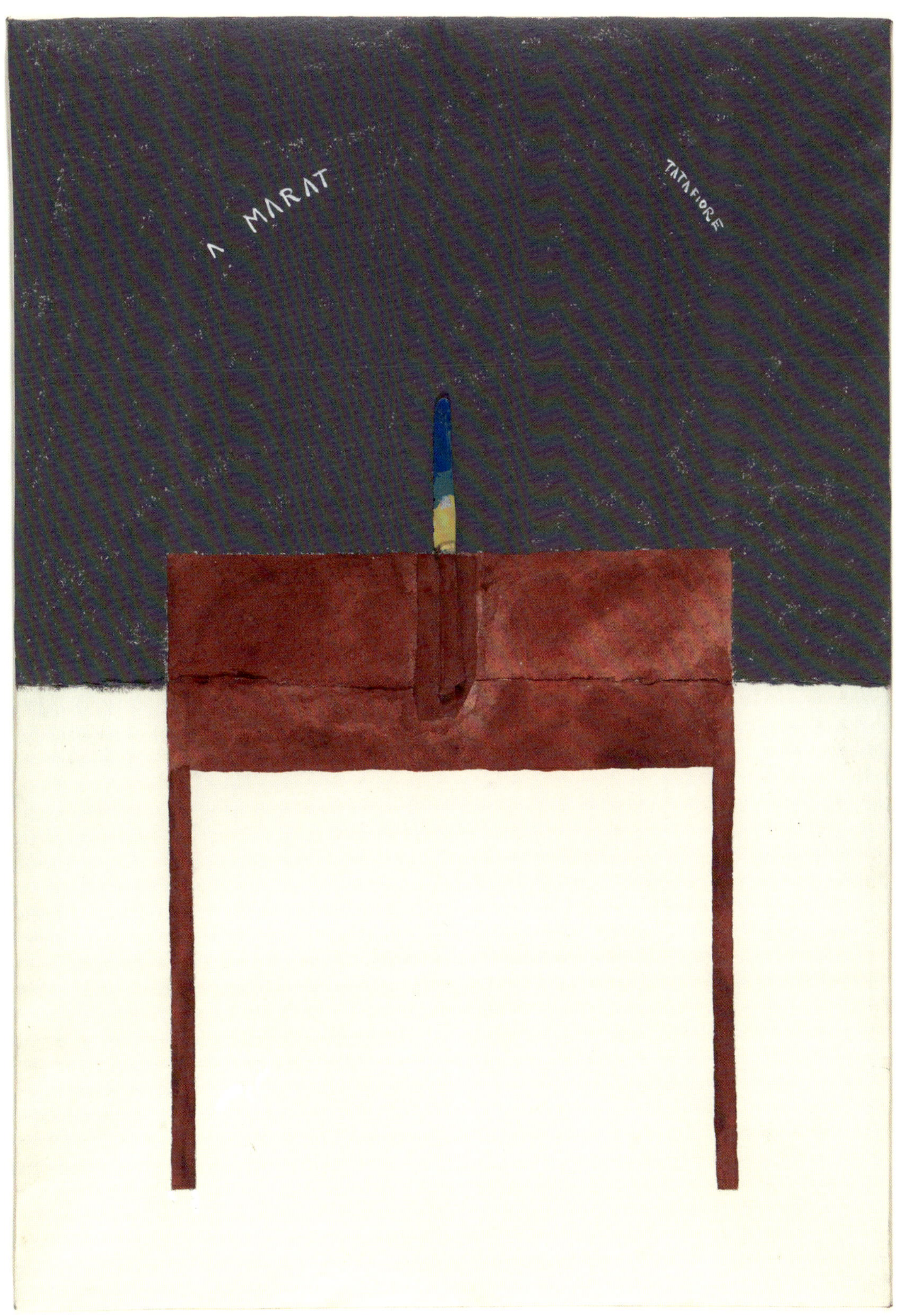

FIG. 34
Ernest Tatafiore, *To Marat*, [1989], mixed technique on paper, 100 × 70 cm.
Brussels, Royal Museums of Fine Arts of Belgium, inv. 11013.

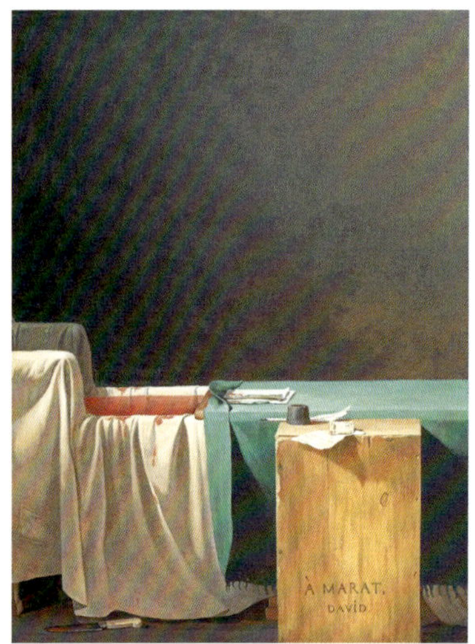

FIG. 35
Yue Minjun, *The Death of Marat*, 2002,
oil on canvas, 292 × 220 cm.
Beijing, private collection.

At once an artist and activist, Ai Weiwei (°1957) knows the price of challenging the Chinese government: in 2011 he was arrested and held incommunicado for two months, sparking an international campaign for his release, whereupon the artist He Xiangyu (°1986) produced a hyper-realistic sculpture in fibreglass representing Ai Weiwei, dressed in the costume of the People's representatives during the Chinese Communist Party congresses, lying as if inanimate, face to the ground, and entitled it *The Death of Marat:* in so doing, he turned his model into a new revolutionary hero [fig. 36]. Exhibited for the first time in a window onto the street at the Balmoral artists' residence in Bad Ems (Germany), the work aroused great excitement, with one citizen going so far as to lodge a complaint with the authorities, considering that it constituted an attack on the dignity of the dead.

He Xiangyu's work would experience a strange fate. In 2016, *India Today* photographer Rohit Chawla produced a black and white image of Ai Weiwei lying on his stomach, his face with closed eyes turned towards the viewer, on a beach in Lesbos. The artist had embarked on a vast journey to alert world opinion to the fate of migrants *en route* to Europe, culminating the following year in the release of his film *HumanFlow*. The photograph aroused deep unease for reproducing the picture of little Alan Kurdi, a three-year-old Syrian refugee found dead in 2015 on a beach at Bodrum in Turkey. But in 2019, Ai Weiwei produced a large tableau made of Lego bricks, reproducing Rohit Chawla's photograph in bright colours, and entitled it *After The Death of Marat* [fig. 37]: By referring to He Xiangyu's sculpture, he may have sought to dismiss the criticisms aimed at him in this episode, and to link the image to his own biography – or, quite simply, to make a direct reference to David's painting.

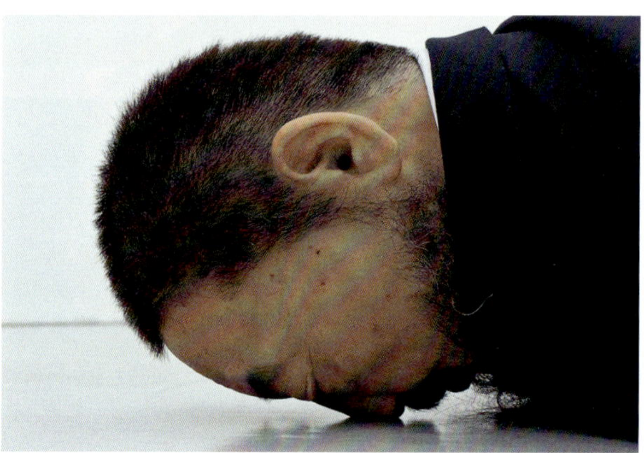

FIG. 36
He Xiangyu, *The Death of Marat*,
2011, fibreglass, silicone,
fabric, human hair and leather,
36 × 183 × 85 cm.
Courtesy of the artist.

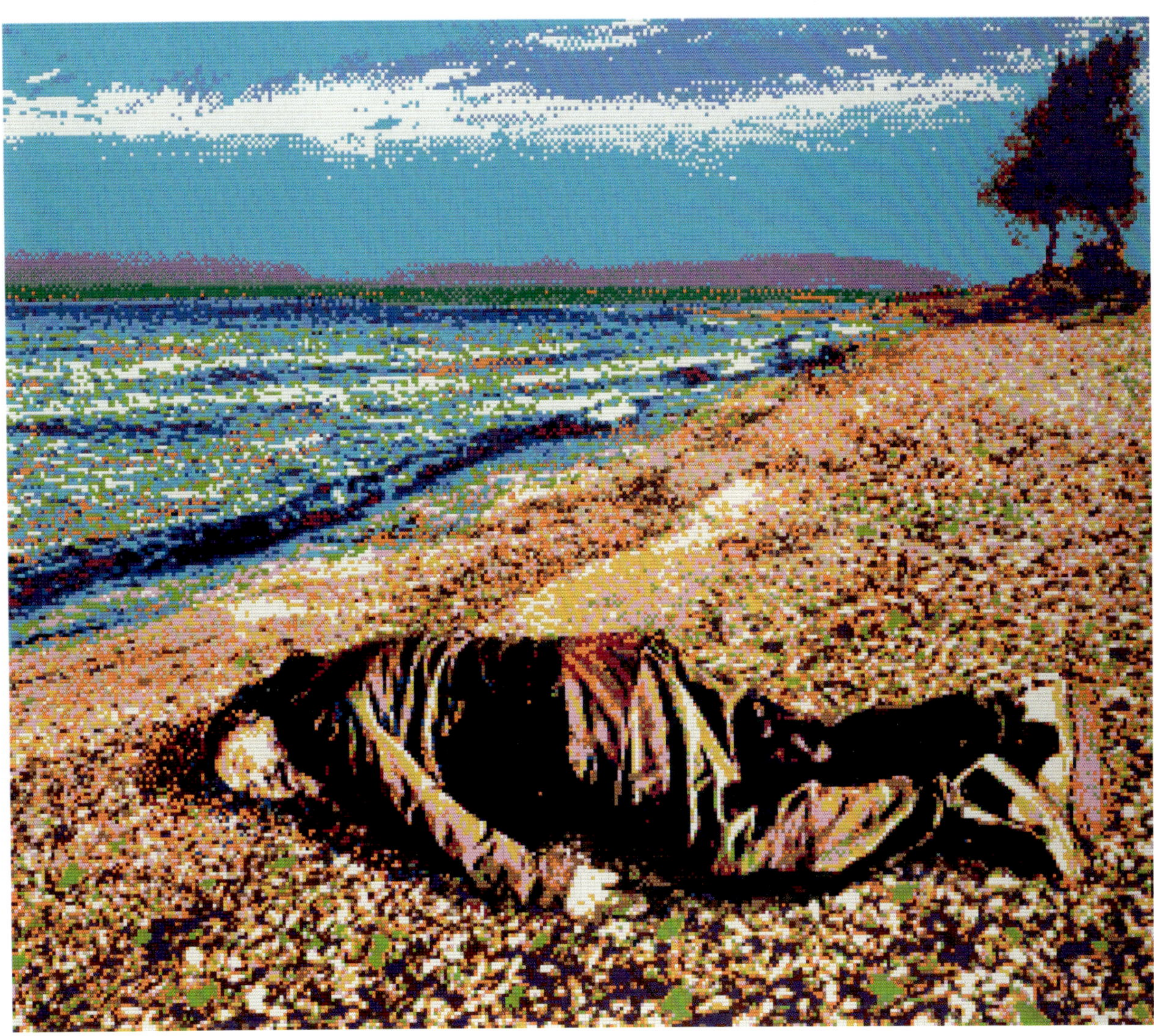

FIG. 37
Ai Weiwei, *After The Death of Marat*, 2019, Lego bricks (edition 1 of 2 + 1 AP), 231 × 269.5 cm. Courtesy of the artist.

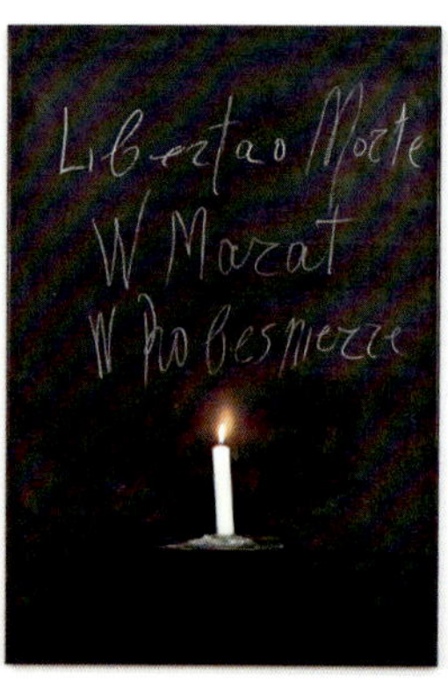

FIG. 38
Jannis Kounellis, untitled *(Libertà o Morte W. Marat W. Robespierre)*, 1969, iron plate, white chalk and candle, 100 × 70 cm. Paris, Monnaie de Paris.

As we have seen, since the beginning of the twentieth century, Jacques-Louis David's masterpiece has aroused, and continues to arouse, a number of interpretations in very diverse registers, whether in the stripped-down style characteristic of the *arte povera* of Jannis Kounellis (1936-2017) (Untitled / *Libertà o Morte W. Marat W. Robespierre*, 1969, and *Death of Marat*, 1974 [fig. 38]), or the spectacular baroque style of Robert (Bob) Wilson (°1941), who transfigures Lady Gaga into Marat in a video tableau accompanied by a soundtrack inspired by the writings of the Marquis de Sade [fig. 39]. The artist recently created and released an NFT (*non-fungible token*) associated with this work: thus Marat, and by proxy Charlotte Corday, are promised eternal life thanks to *blockchain* technology.

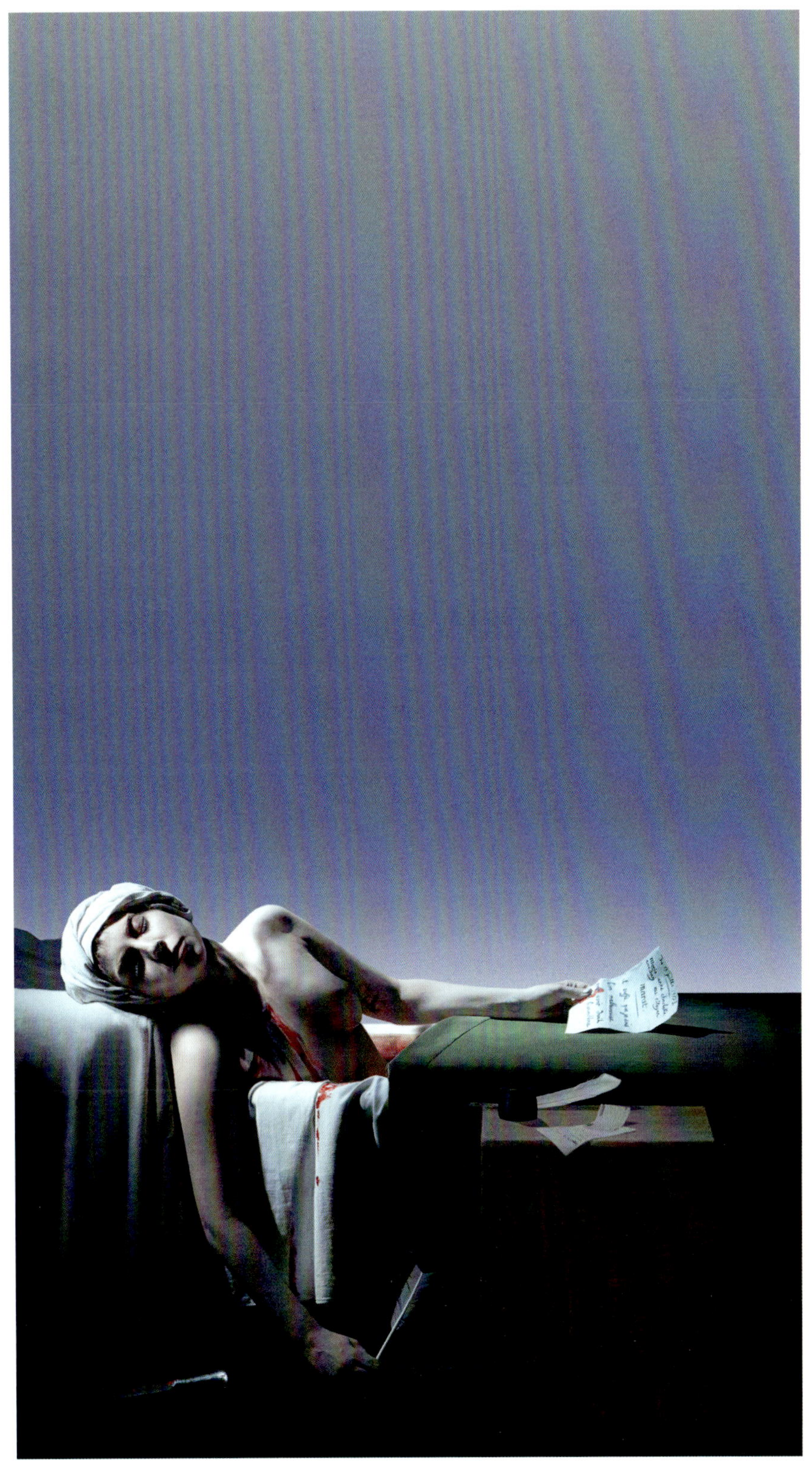

FIG. 39
Robert (Bob) Wilson, *La Mort de Marat*, 2013, video, 12'34", music by Michael Galasso, voice by Lady Gaga, text by Marquis de Sade.
Production: Dissident Industries, Inc., Lumen Arts. Courtesy of RW Work Ltd.

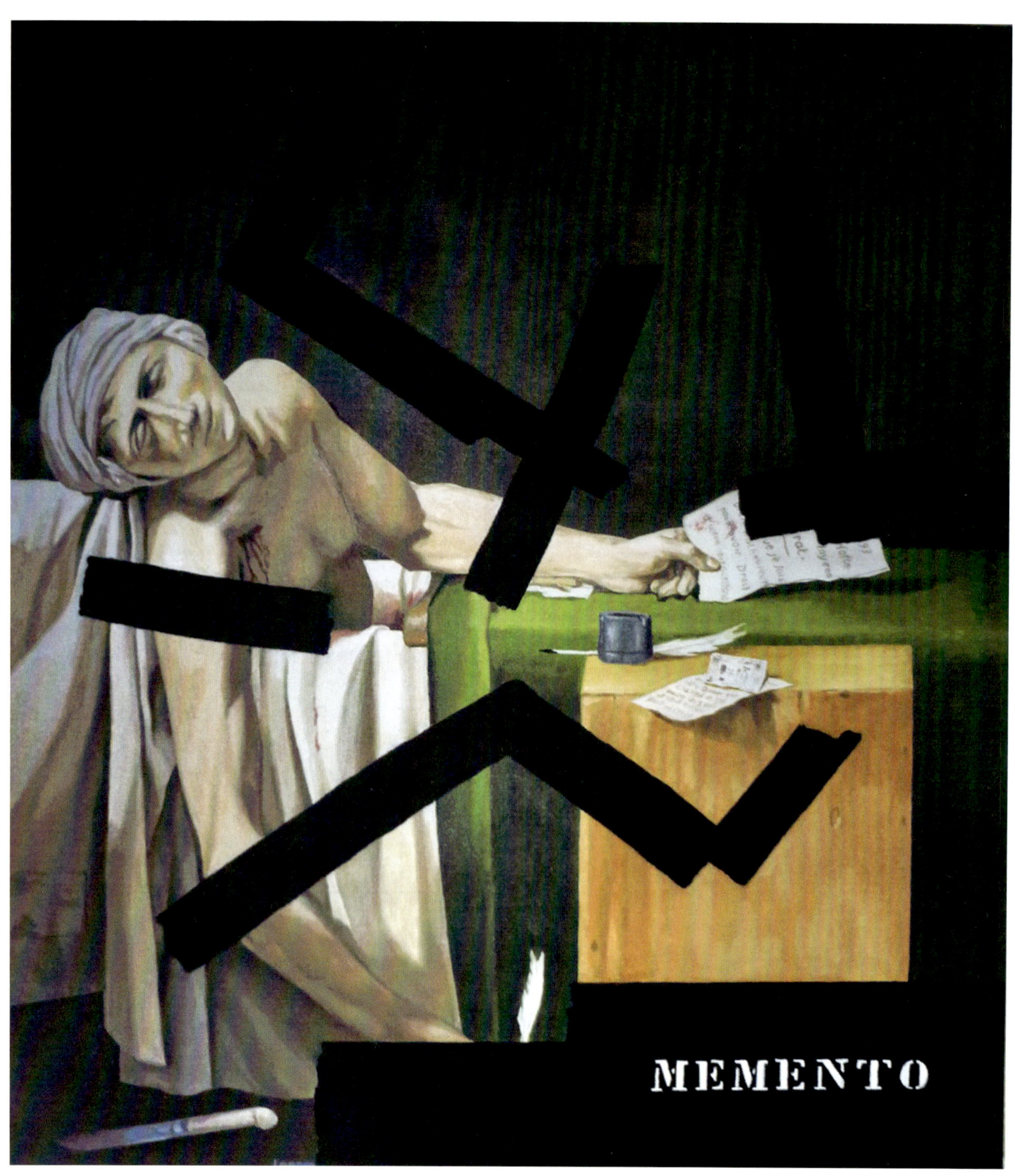

FIG. 40
Jacques Lennep, *Memento (David)*, 2021, oil and acrylic on canvas, 90 × 81 cm. Courtesy of the artist.

Works exhibited

Cat. 1 – fig. 1
Jacques-Louis David
The Death of Marat
1793
Oil on canvas, 165 × 128 cm
Brussels, Royal Museums of Fine Arts of Belgium, bequest of Jules-David Chassagnol, Paris, 1886, inv. 3260

Cat. 2 – fig. 2
Workshop of Jacques-Louis David
The Death of Marat, 13 July 1793
1794
Oil on canvas, 157 × 136 cm
Musée national des Châteaux de Versailles et de Trianon, inv. MV 5608

Cat. 3 – fig. 4
Workshop of Jacques-Louis David
The Death of Marat
After 1793
Oil on canvas, 111.3 × 86.1 cm
Reims, Musée des Beaux-arts, inv. 879.8.1

Cat. 4 – fig. 5
Workshop of Jacques-Louis David
The Death of Marat
Circa 1793
Oil on canvas, 92 × 73 cm
Musée des Beaux-Arts de Dijon, inv. 2306

Cat. 5 – fig. 11
Anonymous
The Death of Marat after David
After 1840
Oil on canvas, 72 × 91 cm
France, private collection

Cat. 6 – fig. 34
Ernesto Tatafiore
À *Marat*
[1989]
Mixed technique on paper, 100 × 70 cm
Brussels, Royal Museums of Fine Arts of Belgium, acquired in 1989, inv. 11013

Cat. 7 – fig. 26
Pablo Picasso
The Murder
1934
Pen, India ink and wash on prepared paper, 34.5 × 51 cm
Paris, Musée national Picasso-Paris, donated in 1979, inv. MP1134

Cat. 8 – fig. 29
Rachel Labastie
Charlotte
2021
Porcelain cameos and chains, oak jewellery box, 190 × 115 × 50 cm
Courtesy of the artist

Cat. 9 – fig. 33
Jan Van Imschoot
La Pénétration inédite
2018
Oil on canvas, 150 × 170 cm
Courtesy the artist and Galerie Templon

Cat. 10 – fig. 22
Jean-Luc Moerman
The Death of Marat
2021
Single copy Chromalux print, 150 × 110 cm
Private collection

Cat. 11 – fig. 32
Gavin Turk
The Death of Marat
1998
Wax, stone, wood and glass showcase, 200 × 170.2 × 250 cm
Private collection

Cat. 12 – fig. 39
Robert Wilson
La Mort de Marat
2013
HD video, music by Michel Galasso, voice by Lady Gaga, texts by the Marquis de Sade
12'34"
Production: Dissident Industries, Inc., Lumen Arts
Courtesy of RW Work Ltd.

Cat. 13 – fig. 37
Ai Weiwei
After "The Death of Marat"
2019
Lego bricks, 231 × 269.5 cm
Courtesy of the artist

Cat. 14 – fig. 40
Jacques Lennep
Memento (David)
2021
Oil and acrylic on canvas, 90 × 81 cm
Courtesy of the artist

Acknowledgements

The Royal Museums of Fine Arts of Belgium would like to thank
the public and private institutions and also the artists and collectors,
who made this exhibition possible by lending their works:

Aeroplastics Gallery, Brussels
Ai Weiwei
Galerie Max Hetzler Berlin | Paris | London
Galerie Templon, Paris - Brussels
Rachel Labastie
Jacques Lennep
Lumen Arts LLC
Jean-Luc Moerman
Musée des Beaux-Arts, Reims
Musée des Beaux-Arts de Dijon
Musée national des Châteaux de Versailles et de Trianon
Musée national Picasso-Paris
Gavin Turk
Jan Van Imschoot
Robert Wilson

As well as all those preferred to remain anonymous.

We would also like to thank all those whose assisted us in our researches,
whose cooperation has been crucial to the realization of the exhibition
and the writing of the present catalogue, in particular
the Centre européen d'Archéométrie at Liège university.

In partnership with:

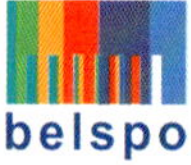

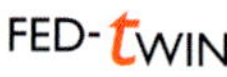

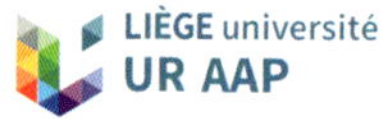

Photographic credits

Every effort has been made to trace copyright holders. If however, you feel that you have inadvertently been overlooked, please contact the publishers.

Brussels, Royal Museum of Fine Arts op Belgium / photo: Johan Geleys – Art Photography: fig. 28, 34; / photo: Centre européen d'Archéométrie, ULiège: fig. 1, 11, 13, 14, 15, 16a, 16b, 18, 19, 20, 21, cover and flap; / photo: Samir Al-Haddad: fig. 12.
Courtesy Galerie Max Hetzler Berlin | Paris | London. Photo: Nicolas Brasseur: fig. 37.
© Courtesy of Gavin Turk / Live Stock Market / photo: Stephen White: fig. 32.
Courtesy He Xiangyu Studio: fig. 36.
Courtesy Yue Minjun Studio: fig. 35.
Dijon, Musée des Beaux-Arts / photo: François Jay: fig. 5, 7.
© Fondation Calvet d'Avignon: fig. 10.
Courtesy Jan Van Imschoot and Galerie Templon / photo: Isabelle Arthuis: fig. 33.
Kendal, Abbot Hall Art Gallery: fig. 27.
© Kristien Daem: fig. 29.
Lyon, Bibliothèque municipale: fig. 9, 16d.
Oslo, Munch Museum: fig. 24.
© Paul Salveson / courtesy Thomas Houseago and Xavier Hufkens, Brussels: fig. 31.
Reims, Musée des Beaux-Arts / photo: Christian Devleeschauwer: fig. 4.
© RMN-Grand Palais (Château de Versailles) / image RMN-GP: fig. 8, 16c.
© RMN-Grand Palais (Château de Versailles) / photo: Franck Raux: fig. 2.
© RMN-Grand Palais (musée du Louvre) / photo: Gérard Blot: fig. 17.
© RMN-Grand Palais (musée du Louvre) / photo: Martine Beck-Coppola: fig. 3.
© RMN-Grand Palais (Musée national Picasso-Paris): photo: Mathieu Rabeau: fig. 23, 25, 26.
© RW Work Ltd.: fig. 39.
© Tate, London: fig. 30.

Front cover:
Jacques-Louis David, *The Death of Marat* (detail), 1793,
oil on canvas, Brussels, Royal Museums of Fine Arts of Belgium, inv. 3260.
Superimposed details:
1) infrared reflectograph of Marat's head, Brussels version;
2) Anonymous, *The Death of Marat (after David)*, after 1840, oil on canvas,
Paris, private collection;
3) Jean-Luc Moerman, *The Death of Marat*, 2021, Chromalux print,
private collection. See pages 5, 12, 15 and 27.

Back cover:
Jacques-Louis David, *The Death of Marat* (detail), 1793,
oil on canvas, Brussels, Royal Museums of Fine Arts of Belgium, inv. 3260.

This book accompanies the exhibition *The Death of Marat* organized at the Royal Museums of Fine Arts of Belgium from 28 April to 7 August 2022. It is published simultaneously in English, French and Dutch.

Exhibition curators
Francisca Vandepitte and Pierre-Yves Desaive
with the collaboration of the Centre européen d'archéométrie, ULiège
Catherine Defeyt and David Strivay

ROYAL MUSEUMS OF FINE ARTS OF BELGIUM

Director General
Michel Draguet
Secretariat of the Director General
Patricia Robeets

Exhibitions Department
Head of Department: Sophie Van Vliet
Project coordination: Josefien Magnus

Conservation
Operational management: Inga Rossi-Schrimpf
Secretariat: Charles Fumunjere
Conservation: Pierre-Yves Desaive, Dominique Marechal, Francisca Vandepitte
Archives and library: Ingrid Goddeeris, Veronique Cardon, Aude Alexandre
Digital museum: Karine Lasaracina, Lies Van de Cappelle, Odile Keromnes, Wouter Paelinck

Support services
General Management: Colette Janssen
Secretariat: Dries van Wielendaele
Human resources: Kristof Sneyers and team
*Financial management:*Sarra Chebrek and team
Informatics: Benoît Lécailler and Miloud El Moussaoui
Security & Facility Management: Maarten Lousbergh
Hard Facilities: Yves Vandeven and team
Soft Facilities and scenography: Thu-Maï Dang and team
Security: Joachim Meert, dispatch service and security team
Technical security expert: Ives Breels
Electricity and lighting: Rudy Cloetens and team
Translation: Lieve Coene

Visitor services
General Management: Isabelle Vanhoonacker
Secretariat: Dilovan Dogan
Communication, press and public relations: Amélie Jennequin, Samir Al-Haddad
Graphic design: Piet Bodyn, Vladimir Tanghe
Cultural mediation & Bespole museum: Isabelle Vanhoonacker and her team
Publications: Fabrice Biasino
Sponsorship and partnerships: Christine Ayoub
Nocturnes and events: Halima El Ouardi
Front Office: Thomas Vanden Dorpe and his team

External collaborators
Transport: Mobull
Insurance: Eeckman Art & Insurance

Publication
Authors: Catherine Defeyt, Pierre-Yves Desaive, Francisca Vandepitte
General coordination, editorial follow-up and iconography: Fabrice Biasino (RMFAB), Alexandra Delabie
Translation: Michael Lomax
Proofreading: Adam Rickards
Graphic design and layout: Nelly Riedel
Photoengraving: Studio 4C, Paris
Printing and binding: GPS
Printed on Magno Volume 150g; texts composed in Sage, Verlag and Walbaum.

Royal Museums of Fine Arts of Belgium
Rue du Musée, 9
B-1000 Brussels
Tel. +32 (0)2 508 32 11
www.fine-arts-museum.be

Éditions mare & martin
Rue Danton 16
F-94 270 Le Kremlin-Bicêtre
Tel. +33(0) +33 0 47 70 70
www.mareetmartin.com

President: Gaël Martin
Editorial Director: Alain Bonnet
Director of Art development: Jean-Louis Fraud
Production Manager: Jessica Clerc

ISBN FR : 978-2-36222-057-9
ISBN UK : 978-2-36222-058-6
ISBN NL : 978-2-36222-056-2

Legal deposit: May 2022
Printed and bound in EU.